The
GREAT GOLF COURSES OF CANADA

Revised and Updated

The
GREAT GOLF COURSES OF CANADA

Revised and Updated

by John Gordon
Photography by Michael French

A FIREFLY BOOK

A FIREFLY BOOK

Front cover photograph of Devil's Pulpit by Doug Ball.

ISBN 1-895565-19-7

Firefly Books Ltd.
250 Sparks Avenue
Willowdale, Ontario, Canada
M2H 2S4

Published in the United States by:
Firefly Books (U.S.) Inc.
Ellicott Station
P.O. Box 1338
Buffalo, NY
14205

Canadian Cataloguing in Publication Data

      Gordon, John (John William)
           The great golf courses of Canada

      ISBN 1-895565-19-7

      1. Golf courses - Canada. I. Title.

      GV975.G67 1993   796.352'06871   C90-094182-0

Printed and bound in Canada by D.W. Friesen Printing

To my family
Leslie, Will and Allie

and

to golf -
after everything else
it is still a game.

ACKNOWLEDGEMENTS

I wish to extend my gratitude and appreciation to the following:

Once again, Bill Ironstone for introducing me to golf; Rex Revere for showing me what it means; Jim Fitchette for his chapters on Banff and Jasper; Bob Weeks for Weston; Mike Rutsey for something or other; and Rob Gilroy, a former colleague at The Canadian Press who has resurfaced as media co-ordinator with the Canadian Tour and provided much-needed research assistance for this revised edition. I have endeavored to credit all sources within the text and apologize for unintentional oversights.

As in the original volume, almost every pro, general manager or other principal at the golf courses contained in this book co-operated to the best of their abilities. Architects such as Tom McBroom and Doug Carrick went to great lengths to continue to educate me in the art of golf course design. Individual members at various clubs also contributed substantially. Chief among these were Gordon Wainwright and R.J. Quinton of Niakwa.

I am also indebted to the Board of Directors of the Canadian Golf Foundation and the Board and Executive Committee of the Royal Canadian Golf Association. Without their forebearance I would not have been able to write this.

My professional admiration goes out to photographer Michael French, whose talents are as evident in the following pages as they were in the first volume. I will always be indebted to my publisher, Jim Williamson, who instigated both ventures and brought them to fruition.

Sincere appreciation goes to all the golfers who bought the first edition, making this volume a necessity.

Finally, here's to my wife Leslie, my son Will and my daughter Allie for putting up with me working weekends and evenings.

TABLE OF CONTENTS

INTRODUCTION

The original volume of The Great Golf Courses of Canada focussed on established courses, most of which had decades of history to recount. This version has retained a representative section of these, but we have chosen a couple of dozen additions. Most of the new courses are exactly that — new — and hole-by-hole descriptions are provided to give a sense of actually playing them. Most have opened in the first couple of years of this decade and represent the state of the art in design and construction techniques.

Several of this new generation of Canadian courses showcase homegrown architects in a manner unprecedented since the heyday of Toronto's Stanley Thompson, some 70 years ago. Just as significantly, some have incorporated rugged Canadian landscape — the Rockies, the Canadian Shield, the Niagara Escarpment — as an integral part of their design. These trends, to my mind at least, represent Canadian golf courses moving toward an identity as distinctive as Scottish links.

These are not necessarily *the* best golf courses in Canada. Instead, they are some of the oldest, some of the newest, some of the toughest, some of the prettiest... In the first volume, I said that selecting golf courses is as subjective as choosing a spouse. I have my favorites: two of which are Glen Abbey, where I work, and Midland Golf and Country Club, a venerable Nicol Thompson design on the shores of Georgian Bay in central Ontario, where I am a member.

You, too, will have a personal bias. While your favorite might not be in here (you will notice I couldn't manage to squeeze in Midland), I hope you will enjoy the tour of a cross-section of some of the world's finest golf courses, right here in Canada.

John Gordon
Spring 1993

Every hole at Banff features the natural beauty of the Rockies.

BANFF SPRINGS

Golf Course

Architects: Stanley Thompson (18)
Bill Robinson (9)
Head Professional: Doug Wood
Manager: Stan Bishop
Superintendent: Bernie Thiesen

Banff Springs, it is said, was the first golf course to cost $1 million to build. The original 18 holes represented a test of man using machinery to mould nature to his purposes rather than fighting it into submission. "Nature must always be the architect's model," said course designer Stanley Thompson. Despite those sentiments, there was no avoiding the fact the thousands of tons of rock had to be blasted and hundreds of trees had to be sacrificed to create this masterpiece which came into being in 1927. So skilful was this act of creation that, in maturity, the course appears one with nature.

Those 18 holes now are labelled the Rundle and Sulphur nines, while another nine, Tunnel, was designed by Bill Robinson of British Columbia and put into play in 1989. "We tried to make it as similar to the old course as we could," Robinson said. The three nines are played in various combinations, but it is the original 18 of which golfers speak with reverence. The setting is unparalleled. In the shadow of Mount Rundle, Sulphur Mountain and Tunnel Mountain, the holes stretch along the Bow River within the confines of Banff National Park. The beauty of the course and the surrounding terrain are breathtaking: pine forests, crystal-clear water, snowy

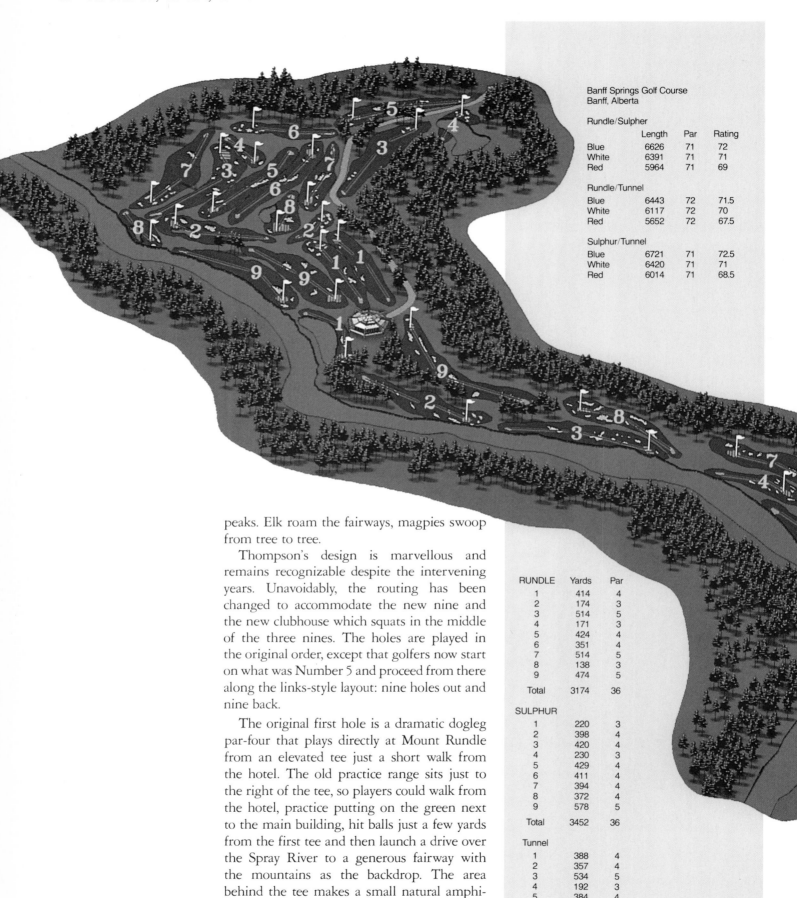

Banff Springs Golf Course
Banff, Alberta

Rundle/Sulpher

	Length	Par	Rating
Blue	6626	71	72
White	6391	71	71
Red	5964	71	69

Rundle/Tunnel

	Length	Par	Rating
Blue	6443	72	71.5
White	6117	72	70
Red	5652	72	67.5

Sulphur/Tunnel

	Length	Par	Rating
Blue	6721	71	72.5
White	6420	71	71
Red	6014	71	68.5

RUNDLE	Yards	Par
1	414	4
2	174	3
3	514	5
4	171	3
5	424	4
6	351	4
7	514	5
8	138	3
9	474	5
Total	3174	36
SULPHUR		
1	220	3
2	398	4
3	420	4
4	230	3
5	429	4
6	411	4
7	394	4
8	372	4
9	578	5
Total	3452	36
Tunnel		
1	388	4
2	357	4
3	534	5
4	192	3
5	384	4
6	474	5
7	382	4
8	134	3
9	424	4
Total	3268	36

peaks. Elk roam the fairways, magpies swoop from tree to tree.

Thompson's design is marvellous and remains recognizable despite the intervening years. Unavoidably, the routing has been changed to accommodate the new nine and the new clubhouse which squats in the middle of the three nines. The holes are played in the original order, except that golfers now start on what was Number 5 and proceed from there along the links-style layout: nine holes out and nine back.

The original first hole is a dramatic dogleg par-four that plays directly at Mount Rundle from an elevated tee just a short walk from the hotel. The old practice range sits just to the right of the tee, so players could walk from the hotel, practice putting on the green next to the main building, hit balls just a few yards from the first tee and then launch a drive over the Spray River to a generous fairway with the mountains as the backdrop. The area behind the tee makes a small natural amphi-theatre where other golfers or guests could watch the proceedings. This fine starting hole now is the 15th.

The former finishing hole (now the 14th,

or the fifth of the Sulphur nine) is a strong dogleg par-four measuring 429 yards from the blues with more than two dozen bunkers all told. Some of these bunkers protect the driving area, some threaten faulty approaches, where others guard three sides of the green. The hole plays into the prevailing wind, so the second shot must often be a fairway wood or long-iron. The magnificent presence of the Banff Springs Hotel looms in the distance: a perfect home hole. With the new arrangement, the finishing hole is the old Number 4, a par-five, and no slouch at 580 yards from the blues with plenty of bunkers, mounds and swales.

The fairways at Banff Springs feature many sweeping contours to make drives and second shots challenging. Many fairways are bordered by mounds that tend to bring off-line drives back into play. Driving areas are moderately wide in most places, but the smart golfer will try to play to a particular location in the fairway to set up a favorable angle to the green. The contouring of the fairways and greens echoes the meandering movement of the Bow River and the surrounding terrain at the base of the mountains.

Most greens are canted toward the approaching golfer to receive incoming shots and many are raised above the level of the fairway. The golfer usually has the option of rolling the ball onto the greens; often the sole approach method for high-handicappers. The greens are not large by modern standards, although their size varies appropriately according to the shot the golfer is expected to play. They have many subtle contours and breaks that make three-footers treacherous, but they are not gimmicky.

The most memorable feature of Banff Springs is the bunkering. Most of the bunkers are located in or on mounds, and they feature flashed faces to make them visible from afar. As one approaches them, they change their shape and appearance, revealing new facets from different angles, just as the appearance of the surrounding mountains changes when seen from different angles or in different light.

Mis-hit approach shots tend to migrate into greenside bunkers, and certain key fairways bunkers also seem to attract off-line balls. Many fairway bunkers serve to catch errant shots and save them from the woods, while others indicate the preferred line: drive over them safely

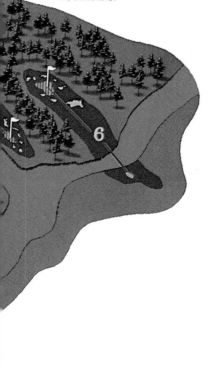

The "Little Bow" — another of Thompson's inspired par-threes.

The famed "Cauldron" at Banff Springs plays 171 yards over a mountain lake.

and you have a good angle for approaching the green. The bunkers are contoured such that the ball tends to roll down the face; one is never confronted with an "impossible" bunker shot.

The most exciting single shot is probably the tee shot at Number 4, the "Devil's Cauldron". The tee is quite elevated compared to the sloping green that is carved into the hillside about 170 yards away. The shot must carry over a glacial lake to the green, a shelf about 15 feet above the water level. Mount Rundle watches on the right. Club selection is tricky here: on a calm day, a smooth eight-iron; in the wind, use your imagination.

Banff's high elevation, more than 1,600 metres above sea level, means that the ball flies farther, perhaps one-to-two clubs' differ-

ence. On the other hand, the wind varies from imperceptible to gale-force, meaning that downwind par-fours in excess of 400 yards can be played driver-wedge. As well, the mountain backdrops tend to distort one's perspective, making the business of judging distances a memorable experience, to say the least. The story is told of Gene Sarazen who ignored the advice of his local caddie, chose a club on his own, and barely made it halfway to the green.

The century-old Banff Springs Hotel, with more than 800 rooms, is a massive edifice that looks like a noble's castle in the Alps. The lobby and parts of the mezzanine are dark with heavy furniture; in places, it looks like a medieval fortress. The "new" addition was built in the 1920s and has recently received multi-million-dollar renovations.

Stanley Thompson was a genius at designing par-threes. Here, the 138-yard "Papoose."

Stanley Thompson (1894-1952)

Stanley Thompson was one of five brothers, all of whom achieved notoriety in golfing circles. Brothers Frank and Bill won the Canadian Amateur, Nicol was the head professional at Hamilton Golf and Country Club and Matt was a pro in Western Canada. Stanley, while a formidable player (he claimed the medalist title in the 1923 Canadian Amateur qualifying with a set of borrowed clubs), would become recognized as the dean of Canadian golf course architects. His memorials range literally from one coast of Canada to the other, from Capilano in West Vancouver to Highlands Links on Cape Breton Island. In between, he created masterpieces such as Jasper Park, Westmount, St. George's and a multitude of others. Banff, one of his crowning achievements, has the dubious distinction of being the first course in the world to cost more than $1 million to build. Thompson was one of three founders of the American Society of Golf Course Architects. The others were Donald Ross and Robert Trent Jones, at one time Thompson's junior partner.

JASPER PARK LODGE

Golf Course

Architect: Stanley Thompson
Head Professional: Ron MacLeod
Manager: Perry Cooper
Superintendent: Brian Hill

Jasper Park's classic 18-hole course was designed by Canada's greatest architect, Stanley Thompson, and opened for play in 1925. This splendid resort is located in Jasper National Park in the heart of the Rockies, just outside the town of Jasper on Lac Beauvert, where the water is green and clear. Nearby looms a range of rugged peaks called the Whistlers. The course winds through pine woods, affording golfers stunning views of the surrounding snow-capped mountains, which form a backdrop for most of the holes. Jasper Park's main challenges are the wind, the undulating fairways, the tricky greens and the fascinating bunkers.

The course sits close to the main lodge and some of the cabins. The practice range is 10 metres from the first tee and it is long enough for Greg Norman's longest drives. The holes move in an essentially circular pattern clockwise. Thus, the golfer's orientation with respect to the wind changes subtly from hole to hole; it is never really the same from one to the next. The course is a pleasant walk, with tees close by previous greens in all instances, and the elevation above sea level (about 1,000 metres) is not so extreme that one becomes winded because of the thin mountain air.

The holes are gently contoured with soft sweeping lines that

are most inviting and interesting to behold. Trees line both sides of many fairways, but landing areas are, for the most part, generous. Still, there are clearly preferred sides of the fairways if one hopes to have an advantageous line into the greens, which themselves tend to be medium-sized to smallish and set at angles to the fairways. They tend to be canted toward the approaching golfer and many are slightly elevated.

The front entrance to every green is open to allow running approach shots. Some greens, however, are raised enough that most successful approaches will fly all the way to the putting surface. The 16th green is guarded in front by water for more than three-quarters of its width; but a running shot to the extreme right side of the fairway could find the putting surface, if played to perfection.

The most notable feature of the course, after the spectacular setting, is Thompson's incomparable bunkering. His use of sand, here and at Banff Springs four hours to the south, could serve as a doctoral course in the fine art of

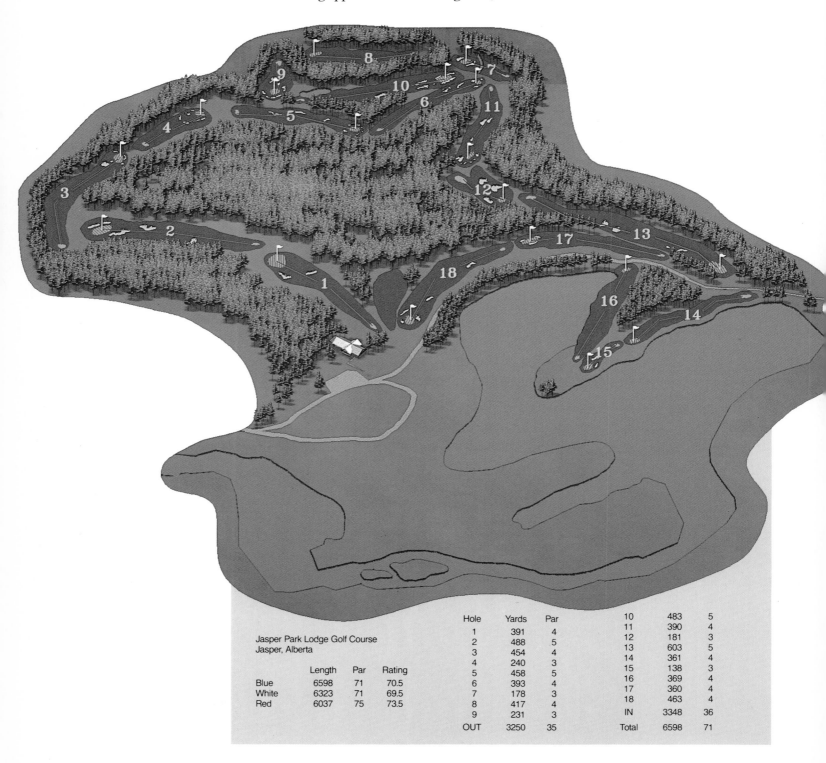

Jasper Park Lodge Golf Course				Hole	Yards	Par			
Jasper, Alberta				1	391	4	10	483	5
				2	488	5	11	390	4
				3	454	4	12	181	3
	Length	Par	Rating	4	240	3	13	603	5
				5	458	5	14	361	4
Blue	6598	71	70.5	6	393	4	15	138	3
White	6323	71	69.5	7	178	3	16	369	4
Red	6037	75	73.5	8	417	4	17	360	4
				9	231	3	18	463	4
				OUT	3250	35	IN	3348	36
							Total	6598	71

bunkering to frame fairways and greens, to provide interesting tactical and strategic challenges, and to enhance the beauty of an already gorgeous setting. The bunkers at Jasper Park are beautifully shaped and their appearance changes depending on the angle from which they are viewed. As you approach them, you see their appearance changing, just as you discover new facets in the surrounding mountains and the lake, every hour, every day.

Many of the bunkers are situated in or on mounds. Sand flashes up their faces so they can be seen from a distance. Some are substantial in depth, but they are gently graded so that errant shots usually finish up in a spot that allows a play toward the hole. Fairway bunkers indicate the line of play and, at some holes, save errant shots from the woods.

The greens are well protected at the sides and backs by bunkers that tend to gather mishit approaches. Several holes feature bunkers that guard the front of the greens but are perhaps 20 or 30 yards short of the actual putting surfaces. This arrangement puts a premium on club selection on approaches, especially as the flashed faces make it appear

that the bunkers are tight to the greens. The greens have many subtle breaks and undulations, in addition to being steeply sloped from back to front in most cases.

The Jasper Park Lodge course is not particularly long, especially given the mountain setting, where the ball tends to carry farther than at sea level: 6,598 yards from the blues, 6,323 from the whites. Par is 71 as there are five par-threes. Thompson provided an excellent range of challenges for each kind of hole. Par-threes measure from 138 to 240 yards from the blues, from 120 to 220 from the whites; the par-fours include three in the 360-yard range and two at 454 and 468 respectively, from the blues. The par-fives range from a reachable 458 yards to a herculean 603. You will need every club in the bag here.

Many of the tees are elevated. The most exciting driving holes are Number 8, where you aim at a distant peak to try to place the ball between large mounds that guard both sides of the fairway; Number 14, a dogleg where the tee is situated on a small point and you cut off as much of the lake as you dare; Number 16 with its tight fairway guarded by water left

Greenside mounds at Jasper Park reflect the varying elevations of the distant mountain peaks.

Mountain streams and lakes join forces with Jasper Park's natural beauty to provide a scenic and sporting delight.

and trees right; and Number 18, a long, downhill dogleg with cavernous bunkers threatening every shot.

The 15th, called "The Bad Baby," is a superb par-three. It measures 138 yards from the blues, 120 from the whites, but it is a tantalizing target. The green is tiny, situated atop a mound with steep sides and a bunker left. Miss this green with your short-iron and you are assured of bogey or worse, especially if you have to pitch across the narrow putting surface. Thompson was unexcelled at designing par-threes.

The golf course is a gem and anyone with an interest in golf history or golf course architecture should find an opportunity to play this classic old course.

The accommodations at Jasper Park Lodge are on par with the course. The resort received the only gold medal awarded in Canada by the U.S. publication, GOLF, in 1989. The main lodge and surrounding cabins contain hundreds of rooms. The main building, built in the early 1950s, is beautiful, airy and peaceful. The floor is made of colorful flagstones; enormous picture windows look out to Lac Beauvert and the Whistlers; two huge fireplaces with hearths you could stand in are the focus of the sitting areas; massive beams and buttresses rise to the ceiling. The decor is tastefully done in every detail, both in the common areas and in the guest rooms. The cuisine and service are excellent and there is a myriad of activities for those few non-golfing hours.

In Love With Cleopatra

The single most memorable shot at Jasper Park Lodge is the tee shot at Number 9, "Cleopatra." A par-three that plays 231 yards from the blues, 214 from the whites, the tee is high on a hill, the green well below and heavily bunkered, sitting atop a mound with steep grassy sides. Choose your weapon, aim at a distant mountain top, and fire away: the drop from tee to green is so great that the ball seems to fly for minutes. The story is told that this hole derived its name as an offshoot of course architect Stanley Thompson's impish humor. Initially, as one stood on this tee, the voluptuous figure of Cleopatra became visible in the outlines of the fairway. Management of the Canadian National Railways, for whom Thompson built the course, persuaded him to disguise some of the contours, although the nickname stuck.

The appropriately named "Maze" is a short but convoluted par-five which starts off the back nine.

The mission at Kananaskis is to offer the green-fee player a private-club experience.

Kananaskis Village, Alberta

KANANASKIS

Country Golf Course

Architect: Robert Trent Jones
Director of Golf: Brian Bygrave
Head Professional: Wayne Bygrave
Superintendent: Jim O'Connor
Manager: Gord Sarkissian

No doubt, when Robert Trent Jones worked with revered Canadian course architect Stanley Thompson on his masterful layout at nearby Banff Springs, he dreamed of the time when he could tackle a similar challenge of his own in the awe-inspiring Rockies. He had to wait 50 years. His chance came in the early 1980s when the Alberta government decided to build a 72-hole golf facility in the Kananaskis River valley near Canmore, an hour west of Calgary.

The massive undertaking was funded by the Alberta Heritage Savings Trust Fund, staked by the province's huge oil production, and stands as a monument to both Jones and the foresight of the provincial government. Two courses, Mount Kidd and Mount Lorette, draw in the neighborhood of 75,000 golfers every season and it is safe to say that very few of that number are disappointed. They may echo Jones' sentiments when he first saw the proposed site: "the finest location I have ever seen for a golf course."

Despite their length — both layouts play to more than 7,000 yards from the tips — Jones provided four sets of tees to ensure that golfers of all abilities could enjoy his creations. Remember, as well, that the thin mountain air allows the ball to fly 10- to 15-per-cent further than at sea level; valuable input for club selection.

The par-three sixth hole on Mount Lorette — you will need a long-iron to a sharply sloping green protected by water.

All in all, Jones remained true to his design philosophy that each hole should be a tough par but an easy bogey.

Mount Kidd gives you little time to collect your wits before presenting what is rated the most difficult hole of its 18. The second hole is a par-five that stretches 536 yards from the white tees, usually into the wind. Take a moment on this tee to appreciate the green oasis that presents itself vividly against the grey granite backdrop of sheer mountain faces. Once back to reality, take care to avoid the righthand fairway bunkers with your tee shot and the river that edges up on the left as you approach the green. Four bunkers protect the relatively small green.

After negotiating the fourth hole, a par-three with a semi-island green that requires from a seven-iron to a four-iron with the wind at your back, you can start to anticipate the sixth. This challenging par-five is not overly long at 484 yards from the whites, but keeping the ball on the fairway is essential. The ideal landing spot is right, but that area is the location of a fairway bunker which complicates matters. A creek runs up the entire left side before looping behind the green and draining into a pond right of the putting surface. Dense

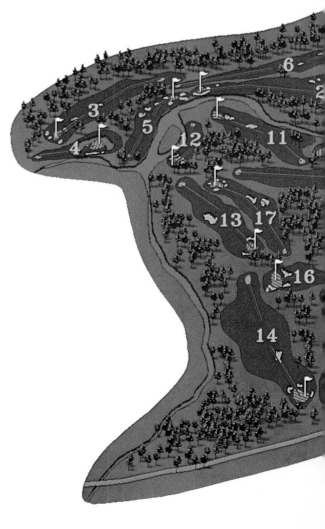

forest guards the left boundary. The intelligent player will lay up in front of this tiered green.

Even taking the thin air into account, the finishing hole of Mount Kidd would make the longest hitters shudder. From the back tees, this hole is 642 yards, but the breathtaking scenery makes every moment spent here worthwhile. It has all the elements which characterize Kananaskis Country: dark-green forest, snow-capped mountains, shimmering water. Hit the tee shot as far as you can, bisect the fairway bunkers with a fairway wood on your second shot, place your mid- to short-iron approach on the right side of the pin, and you will be assured of a successful completion to your round.

Kananaskis Country Golf Course
Kananaskis Village, Alberta

Kidd	Length	Par	Rating
Gold	7049	72	74.5
Blue	6604	72	72
White	6068	72	69/74.5
Red	5539	72	66.5/71.5

Lorette	Length	Par	Rating
Gold	7102	72	74
Blue	6643	72	72
White	6155	72	69/76
Red	5429	72	64.5/72

Mount Kidd Course				Mount Lorette Course		
Hole	Yards	Par		Hole	Yards	Par
1	455	4		1	412	4
2	615	5		2	416	4
3	437	4		3	395	4
4	197	3		4	254	3
5	339	4		5	541	5
6	553	5		6	195	3
7	415	4		7	482	4
8	183	3		8	408	4
9	408	4		9	560	5
OUT	3602	36		OUT	3663	36
10	405	4		10	402	4
11	355	4		11	497	5
12	183	3		12	394	4
13	392	4		13	407	4
14	491	5		14	523	5
15	402	4		15	188	3
16	207	3		16	380	4
17	370	4		17	185	3
18	642	5		18	463	4
IN	3447	36		IN	3439	36
Total	7049	72		Total	7102	72

Even facing as challenging a hole as Mount Lorette's 17th, it is almost impossible to ignore the splendid surroundings.

Moving on to Mount Lorette, you have a slightly more hospitable welcome than at Mount Kidd. The Number 1 rated hole doesn't appear until the fifth tee. At 478 yards, this par-five doesn't test the player's length, but accuracy is a must. A small creek cuts in front of the tee and continues through trees on the left before looping around and embracing the green on three sides. The tee shot must avoid the left fairway bunkers and the brave second shot, if going for the narrow kidney-shaped green in two, should be a faded fairway wood. Be wary of the hidden pond right of the green. Those less confident, or more sensible, should plan to lay up and hope for par.

Many players consider the seventh hole, a 439-yard par-four when played from the blues, the best on the course. Your drive must carry a large pond and stay out of fairway traps which litter the middle and left of the landing area. Being right of these is a mixed blessing because

the pond threatens that side. Those who are fortunate enough to avoid these hazards still must launch a long-iron into a well-bunkered, wavy green.

Touted as the most beautiful hole at Mount Lorette, the par-three 17th reminds the visitor why mountain golf in Canada is special. Lodge-pole pines direct your gaze at the mountains, and the Kananaskis River lies between tee and green, defined by three shimmering white sand traps.

The perfect outing at Kananaskis Country would be to play both courses in the same day, and it's not impossible because a round should not take longer than 4 1/2 hours. Golfers who complete 18 holes in less than that time are presented with a memento by the management. Kan-Alta Golf Management Ltd., which operates the facility under contract, promises to give public golfers a private-club experience and it's a credo they abide by.

Designer Robert Trent Jones called Kananaskis (opposite page) "the finest location I have ever seen for a golf course".

Small greens and little room for bailing out make Wolf Creek a test for even the best player's accuracy.

—————— *Ponoka, Alberta* ——————

WOLF CREEK

Golf Resort

Architect: Rod Whitman
Director of Golf: Ryan Vold
Superintendent: Rick David
Manager: Randy Dool

Wolf Creek is where Canada meets Scotland. Not geographically, of course, but where else would you find a links-style course that uses bleached cattle skulls for 150-yard markers?

Credit Ryan Vold and Rod Whitman with the audacity to dream up Wolf Creek and the perseverance to see it come to fruition in 1984. Vold, a member of the Canadian Professional Golfers' Association, saw the potential for a unique golf course on a portion of his family's ranch south of Edmonton. Conveniently, his friend Whitman had apprenticed under famed U.S. course architect Pete Dye. Whitman surveyed the dunes covered with waving native grasses and wildflowers and visualized a tribute to the origins of golf, set in the Canadian West.

Links-style holes, complete with unmaintained rough and enormous waste bunkers, make up a large part of the Wolf's character. Other holes are lined with trees and provide a contrast to the undulating dunes. Although the scorecard reveals a total length of less than 6,600 yards from the tips, Wolf Creek ravages less-than-competent players who dare to play from the back tees. The scorecard advises that only those with a handicap of five or less should attempt the full length, while those who carry a handicap of 16 or higher should step up to the whites.

As the site of the Canadian Tour's Alberta Open, the course has been the recipient of some glowing reviews. Tour Commissioner Bob Beauchemin heads the list when he sums up what his players thought of the course: "To a man, every player has mentioned what a fair, intriguing, difficult, challenging, fun course it is to play. And there are very few courses where you get that kind of unanimous opinion." Prominent Tour player Matt Cole of Windsor, Ontario, concurs: "You can't get nonchalant over one shot — not one drive, not one iron, not one putt." And veteran Canadian pro Bob Panasik harks back to the history of the game, saying, "This is my conception of how golf started. It's a unique golf course in our country."

You get the full impact of that uniqueness

The semi-island green on No. 4 is a real challenge. A ball hit to the back of the island is almost impossible to stop.

from the time you drive into the parking lot. A 20,000-square-foot solid log clubhouse is hunkered down against the wind that sweeps across the Prairies and plays havoc with delicate approach shots.

Wolf Creek spares no mercy for those who do not come prepared to play. "If you can get through the first four or five holes," says Vold, "you've got it made. Number 2 and four kill more people in tournaments than you can believe."

The opening hole is a dogleg-right with spruce trees guarding the lefthand side and massive mounds defining the right. If you hit the landing area, an eight- or nine-iron should get you to the heavily undulating green. Like many approaches at Wolf Creek, this shot can be played two ways: a bump-and-run during

Designer Rod Whitman used Alberta's natural contours to produce remarkable holes such as the par-five 11th.

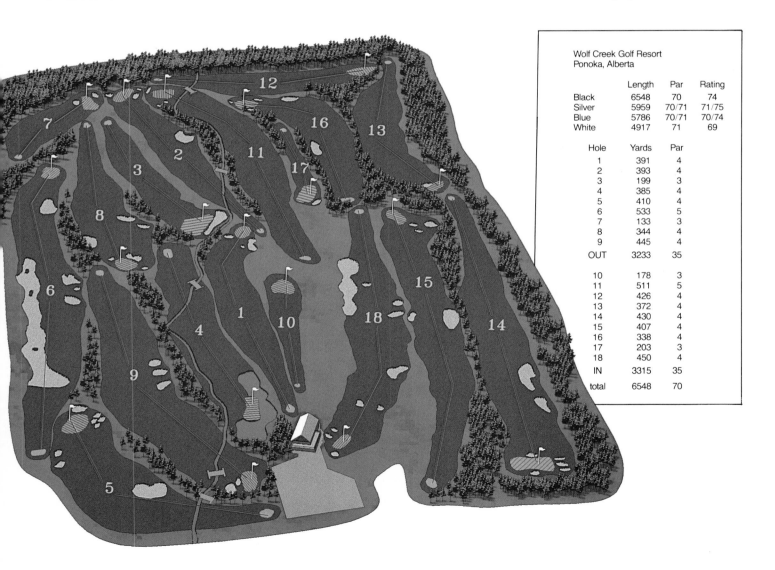

Wolf Creek Golf Resort
Ponoka, Alberta

	Length	Par	Rating
Black	6548	70	74
Silver	5959	70/71	71/75
Blue	5786	70/71	70/74
White	4917	71	69

Hole	Yards	Par
1	391	4
2	393	4
3	199	3
4	385	4
5	410	4
6	533	5
7	133	3
8	344	4
9	445	4
OUT	3233	35
10	178	3
11	511	5
12	426	4
13	372	4
14	430	4
15	407	4
16	338	4
17	203	3
18	450	4
IN	3315	35
total	6548	70

dry weather, or a high short-iron during wet spells.

On Number 2, you must negotiate your tee shot through a tree-lined chute to a landing area 230 yards out from the back tees. The two-tiered green is protected by a sod-walled bunker directly in front. The third hole is a 199-yard par-three that requires anything from a one- to a six-iron depending on the ever-present wind. A very natural hole, again, lined with spruces with a green that runs right to left.

From the elevated tees of Hawk's Alley, the par-four fourth hole, use a three- or four-wood to blast the ball between black spruces. Wolf Creek, the body of water, defines the left boundary of the hole before coming back into play in a most dramatic way: it surrounds the semi-island green. "This is a very severe green," says Vold. "Drop down one club on your approach and run the ball onto the green. If you fly it into the green and hit the downslope on the back level, you just might find yourself in the pond."

Don't think just because you've survived the first four or five holes that your work at Wolf Creek is done. Number 9 has claimed some good golfers and Vold calls holes 11 through 13 "our Amen Corner," referring to the tough holes at Augusta National, site of The Masters tournament.

Buffalo Jump, the par-five 11th hole, is a dogleg-left with a creek running in front of the green. If you are 210 yards or less to the green on your second shot, go for it. Otherwise, lay up and appreciate the naturalness of Whitman's characteristic "potato-chip" greens which flow right into the natural surrounding mounds.

Touring pro Brad King was leading the 1988 Alberta Open when he came to Number 12. When he stepped off the green, he had dropped entirely from the leaderboard after carding a 12. "Any hole at Wolf Creek can do that to you," says Vold. "You have to keep your focus all the way around. Don't fall asleep or it will grab you." The 12th is relatively unprepossessing; the dogleg-left simply requires that you stay out of the woods. Of course, there is a slight matter, hardly worth mentioning, of why they call this hole The Gorge. You must carry this ravine about 175 yards out to reach

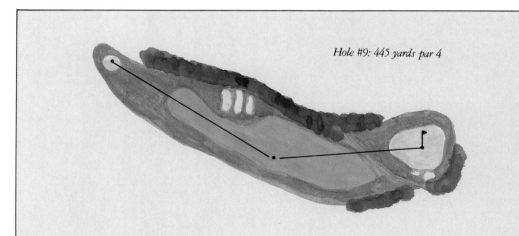

Hole #9: 445 yards par 4

A Heap of Trouble

The ninth hole at Wolf Creek may rank as only the third-toughest handicap hole on the course, but to at least a couple of Canadian Tour pros, there is no doubt it should be Number 1. During the 1990 Alberta Open, the 445-yard par-four claimed two victims in outrageous fashion. The hole calls for a long drive followed by a second shot over a ravine that features a creek and trees on either side. The green is not noted for being receptive to anything but a perfect approach. Toronto's Jack Kay Jr., a young pro with great talent who has played on the U.S. PGA Tour, thought he had it all together as he stepped onto the ninth tee. Twelve shots later, his ball collapsed with relief into the hole. One of Kay's compatriots, whose identity we are sworn not to reveal, took 14 whacks to complete this hole. He walked from the ninth green directly to his car, drove away and never looked back.

the landing area. Hit a fairway wood to the right side of the fairway.

The 13th hole completes this stretch. A drive to the upper deck on this dogleg-left leaves you only a short-iron into a flat green, half of which is hidden behind a steep-walled bunker.

Another nine holes, designed by Whitman in a similar, though even more natural, style were completed in 1990.

You must clear "The Gorge" on your way to parring the par-four 12th.

Often called one of the world's most scenic courses, Capilano sits high above the port city of Vancouver.

—West Vancouver, British Columbia—

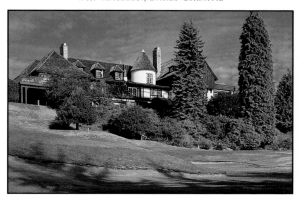

CAPILANO

Golf and Country Club

Architect: Stanley Thompson
Head Professional: Gerry Chatelain
General Manager: Rob Cowan

Understandably, many first-time visitors to Capilano find it hard to concentrate on playing one of Stanley Thompson's finest creations because they are so awed by its spectacular setting. Capilano Golf and Country Club, nestled in the mountains overlooking the beautiful harbor city of Vancouver, is no doubt the most scenic golf course in this country, and must be in the Top 10 in the world in that category. But those novices will soon realize that the demands the course makes on their visual senses will be equalled by the demands on their golfing abilities.

"Visually, it's a gorgeous course," says PGA Tour pro Jim Nelford, who grew up on the West Coast and who has played around the world. "The course is cut right out of the forest. It's away from the city, above the smog. When you get on the first tee, you get a view of all of Vancouver. You just look down the hill and the city is laid out in front of you. And then when you're through playing, it's a real pleasure to go into the clubhouse, which is a grand old thing that sits way on top of everything. You can see the last five holes from the clubhouse, as well as the first hole and the 13th green. What a breathtaking view from up there. Capilano is an old course with plenty of class. . . . One of the best courses I've ever played."

*Capilano's very private enclave
in the hills of West Vancouver
offers a memorable golfing experience for pro or amateur.*

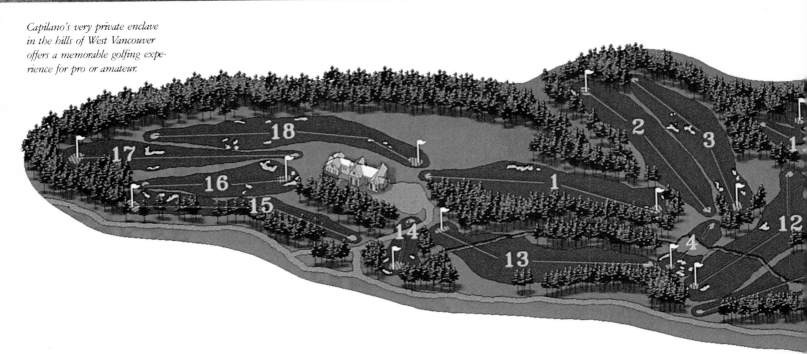

This unparalleled experience grew from the vision and determination of A.J.T. Taylor, an investment broker who was born on Vancouver Island in 1887, and is indelibly linked with the development of West Vancouver itself. Taylor negotiated the purchase of 6,000 acres (at $20 an acre) across the inlet from Vancouver, offering wealthy Britons a land development opportunity. The area, still known as the British Properties and one of the most prestigious locales in the region, at the time was linked with Vancouver only by slow, unreliable ferries. Taylor, using the financial clout of the Guinness Brewing Co., a major investor in the British Properties, bullied through the building of a bridge to the city. The Lions Gate Bridge cost $5.7 million and was the second-longest suspension bridge in the world at the time, trailing only San Francisco's Golden Gate Bridge.

Auspiciously, the bridge was opened by King George VI in 1939, the same year as the clubhouse at Capilano Golf and Country Club, the jewel in the British Properties crown. Seven years earlier, Taylor had enlisted the outstanding Canadian course architect Stanley Thompson to design a layout on Hollyburn Mountain west of the Capilano River. (Thompson received less than $7,000, including fees, plans and expenses, for his labors.)

"We feel hopeful that this project may prove our best endeavor on this continent," says Thompson in correspondence to the course developers. Considering Thompson's body of work, that was a tall, but prophetic, statement. That the course has remained largely unchanged from that original design is testimony to Thompson's abilities and a tribute to an intelligent membership with a continuing deep understanding of the game.

Jock McKinnon, who was the revered head professional here for 42 years, put it this way: "Capilano was and still is a tribute to the architectural genius of Stanley Thompson. There is no need for any tampering apart from taking care of the normal wear and tear. The members have a work of art in their care and possession. My advice is that they should never permit this to be spoiled by people who come along as they have done, and will, and suggest changes at great cost in what I think is a useless attempt to improve a great golf course."

Capilano has had an illustrious membership. In 1937, one year after the course opened, the country's top-ranked amateur arrived and and stayed to make an indelible impression on the club's stately and sensible development. Ken Black, then 26 years old, won the 1939 Canadian Amateur and was made one of the club's first honorary members. He did not play in another national championship until 1946 (the tournament was suspended during the war years) and, much like another famed amateur, Bobby Jones, retired from competitive golf prematurely. Only 34, he became very active in club affairs and is regarded as a guiding

Capilano Golf and Country Club
West Vancouver, British Columbia

	Length	Par	Rating
Blue	6578	72	72
White	6274	72	70
Yellow	5964	74	74

Hole	Yards	Par
1	482	5
2	400	4
3	467	5
4	172	3
5	520	5
6	394	4
7	426	4
8	381	4
9	176	3
OUT	3418	37
10	434	5
11	165	3
12	368	4
13	400	4
14	130	3
15	430	4
16	247	3
17	425	4
18	557	5
IN	3156	35
Total	6574	72

Towering evergreens line Capilano's fairways and make accuracy a must.

light. Other members have claimed national titles and Capilano has played host to innumerable tournaments at all levels.

The club has also been a gracious host to an international who's who, ranging from Bob Hope, Bing Crosby and Billy Graham, to heads of state such as the prime ministers of Japan and Malaysia. In 1971, the clubhouse was the site of a notable wedding reception, that of Pierre and Margaret Trudeau.

"Apart from its natural beauty, this is an ideal golf course," says former Masters champion George Archer, now a standout on the Seniors Tour, "because it is a fair test for the members from the middle tees, and is easily transformed into an excellent championship course from the back tees without tricking up the greens or the rough or the approaches."

To get the best from your round at Capilano, "get your birdies early," says Head Professional Gerry Chatelain. There are three reachable par-fives in the first five holes here, offering an opportunity to gain a couple of strokes from par. The test may come right after those five holes, on the relatively undemanding sixth hole. This short par-four, a drive and a wedge

for most players, has proved to be the most difficult hole in many of the tournaments played here, says Chatelain. To get your four, hit an iron off the tee into the narrow landing area; above all, don't miss the fairway.

Holes seven and eight also claim their share of victims. On the seventh, the Number 1 stroke hole at Capilano, a drive into a gully leaves you with any combination of uneven lies. From there, you hit through a very narrow entrance to a difficult green. Number 8 shares some characteristics with the preceding hole: a shortish par-four with a well-protected green, and a predilection for bogeys.

Once you reach the final four holes, you may regret not having heeded Chatelain's advice about concentrating on those early birdie chances. Capilano's strong finishing holes start at the dogleg-left, par-four 15th, which is followed by a 250-yard par-three. The 17th hole is another strong par-four. The final hole is a tough par-five that features a blind shot into the largest green on the golf course, meaning the emphasis is on correct club selection. The green is on a plateau and protected by bunkers.

Jock McKinnon's Eclectic Record

Jock McKinnon, Capilano's head pro for 42 years, was a fine player in his own right. He is in the record book, however, for a golfing feat that may never be equalled: an eclectic score of 33, recognized by the Guinness Book of World Records. An eclectic score is the sum of a player's all-time personal low scores for each hole on one course, and McKinnon's record is 33, accomplished over 21 years. His eclectic scorecard looks like this:

222 122 221 — 16
212 212 223 — 17

This astounding 39-under-par figure consists of four double-eagles, 18 eagles and one birdie. In Eric Whitehead's excellent book on Capilano, "Hathstauwk", it is noted that McKinnon started this streak during the first round he ever played on the course, just a few weeks after his arrival from Scotland in 1937.

The finishing holes at Capilano have represented the turning point in many tournaments.

*Good course management calls
for a three-wood off the 12th tee.*

MORNINGSTAR

International Golf Course

*Architect: Les Furber
General Manager: Deborah Zorkin
Head Professional: Joe Brien
Superintendent: Richard Donaldson*

The "International" in the official title of this spectacular course on Vancouver Island owes much, as does the very existence of the facility, to businessman Mladen Zorkin.

Zorkin, the farsighted mastermind behind this $20-million, 400-acre golf course/residential development which opened in 1991, was born in 1914 on the island of Dalmatia in the Balkans. He is reputed to speak 11 languages and served as a translator during the Second World War.

When the war ended, Zorkin was in London, England, when he stumbled across a book which contained "The Report of the British Admiralty of 1895." The report, says the urbane, debonair Zorkin, "mentioned the two best climates in the British Empire. One was in New Zealand and the other was the French Creek area around Parksville-Qualicum on Vancouver Island." The report mentioned no freezing for 365 days a year, 22 inches of rain and more than 2,000 hours of sunshine.

Although he arrived in Canada a couple of years later, it wasn't until 1961 that he made his way to his final destination. Now considered one of the most influential developers on the Island, his first venture 30 years ago was the 300-acre Columbia Estates development.

Morningstar Golf Course Parksville, B.C.			
	Length	Par	Rating
Gold	7018	72	74
Blue	6385	72	71
White	5882	72	68
Red	5313	72	65
Hole	Yards		Par
1	378		4
2	388		4
3	508		5
4	232		3
5	436		4
6	460		4
7	464		4
8	190		3
9	538		5
OUT	3594		36

A workaholic, Zorkin doesn't even play golf, but he was shrewd enough to realize how addictive the game can be. "Once you get into golf, you can't get out," he observes. Zorkin himself was hooked on the concept of a world-class golf course when he conceived the project in the 1960s. "People said we were crazy; we could have quit many times," he recalls. But his formula for success, proven many times over, is deceptively simple: "You always have to have the best location and the best facility and you can't fail. What you need is knowledge, ability, perseverance – and a good idea."

Obviously, Morningstar International Golf Course was a good idea: he has been offered $25 million for the facility by a group of offshore investors who wanted to make it an exclusive private enclave. "I would never sell the course because it would defeat the purpose," Zorkin says. "This is a golf course for everybody, not just for Vancouver Island, but for all of North America. My goal is to make Morningstar the best golf course in North America."

True to his word, it cost just $31 to play this public masterpiece in 1992. And the players who came here from around the globe to compete for a spot on the Canadian Professional Golf Tour at the 1992 qualifying school were unanimous in their assessment of Morningstar as "world class."

Zorkin's daughter, Deborah, is Morningstar's general manager and the golfer in the family. "We want to make it one of the top courses in North America, but we want to make it available to everybody. We can play it very hard (the course exceeds 7,000 yards from the back tees), or we can play it very reasonable, having our four and five tee block system. We want to show that we can have a first-class golf course that doesn't get burdened down with a membership. That's a real asset to tourism in the area."

Just as Zorkin makes an indelible impression on anyone he meets, he wants to ensure that every aspect of his course burns itself into a visitor's memory. The word

10	519	5
11	371	4
12	404	4
13	507	5
14	215	3
15	329	4
16	398	4
17	207	3
18	474	4
IN	3424	36
Total	7018	72

"Morningstar" stands in massive five-foot-high letters carved from granite between the first and 10th holes. "It cost me $2,000 a letter and it's 95 feet long. Anyone who comes here will never forget it."

Head pro Joe O'Brien agrees that a visit to Morningstar is unforgettable for a number of reasons. From a golfer's standpoint, O'Brien makes the following observations:

"Morningstar possesses a blend of links-style holes, open fairways and greenside bunkers. The fairways on many holes are completely isolated by trees, requiring straight, strategically placed shots in order to have a clear approach to the greens. It is rare that a day should pass without seeing a deer run across a fairway or one of the resident eagles soaring overhead."

O'Brien also offers some tips to the first-timer at Morningstar in a handy course guide available in the well-stocked pro shop. The first and most important is to manage your game well, playing intelligent shots to the appropriate spots on the fairway. The unforgiving towering trees which line almost every fairway will penalize the foolhardy.

The holes near the clubhouse are rela-

Number 17 offers water down the right side and a very tricky green.

The narrow fifth fairway at Morningstar demands accuracy.

tively open but almost every other hole on the course is cut out of the dense forest. The entire region is presided over by the Coastal Mountains, providing every shot at Morningstar with a breathtaking backdrop.

The area around Morningstar is fast becoming Canada's retirement capital. With year-round golf available to all residents, Morningstar offers a lifestyle previously thought to be found only in more southern climates. The housing development, covering 200 acres, will offer only 500 single-family homes in a forest setting only a five-minute walk from the Pacific Ocean. Once again, it appears the remarkable Dr. Zorkin has a jump on the competition!

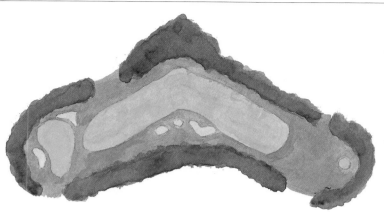

The Toughest Hole at Morningstar

The seventh hole at Morningstar is rated the toughest on the course. It's a long dogleg-left which plays to 464 yards from the gold tees, 434 from the blues, 406 from the whites and 374 from the red blocks. The ideal tee shot is long and straight down the right side of the fairway to avoid the cluster of fairway bunkers on the left, in the corner of the dogleg. A fairway wood or long iron must be struck perfectly to get to the 6,000-square-foot green which is guarded by bunkers. A par 4 here is remarkable.

Number 9, a double-dogleg par 5, has it all: length, lakes, hollows and bunkers.

*Number 18 is a great par
5 that snakes its way back
to the clubbouse.*

Victoria, British Columbia

OLYMPIC VIEW

Golf Club

Architect: *Bill Robinson*
Director of Golf: *Earl Davies*
Head Professional: *Doug Mahovlic*
General Manager: *Bill Lang*
Superintendent: *Randy Page*

It takes exceptional vision to look at a special piece of property and imagine releasing the golf course within. Fred Mathes had that vision in 1988.

Mathes had been given the task of shaping a course from 120 acres of Vancouver Island bush and rock just 20 minutes from the inner harbor of Victoria, British Columbia's captivatingly beautiful capital city.

"It was a jungle," he recalls. "You would not have believed your eyes when we first started. You could only see 20 feet in front of yourself. We crawled around on hands and knees with a compass and measuring tape. We did it hole by hole...we spent hundreds of hours in there. But in the end it is very rewarding."

The result is spectacular and, although some changes were unavoidable in order to clear fairways, earthmoving and clearing were kept to a minimum. The result is a relatively natural, albeit spectacular, course carved out of the forest. Of course, architect Bill Robinson, known for his other designs including Gallagher's Canyon in B.C.'s Interior, contributed his special magic along the way. Aside from calling the site "absolutely the best piece of property I've ever had to work with," Robinson is sure Olympic

*The opening hole — a shotmaker's par 4
with a view of the Olympic Mountains.*

Olympic View Golf Club
Victoria, British Columbia

	Length	Par	Rating
Blue	6475	72	72
White	6071	72	70
Red	5447	72	67
Yellow	5185	72	70.5 (L)

Hole	Yards	Par		Yards	Par
1	378	4	10	320	4
2	330	4	11	130	3
3	562	5	12	335	4
4	153	3	13	595	5
5	366	4	14	407	4
6	238	3	15	382	4
7	333	4	16	107	3
8	420	4	17	417	4
9	467	5	18	535	5
OUT	3247	36	IN	3228	36
			Total	6475	72

View will be rated in the top five in Canada within five years.

Certainly, Mathes et al have done many things right with this semi-private facility which opened in 1990. It is not overly long, yet requires precise shotmaking and calls for every club in the bag. It is open to the public at a time when demand for good golf is at a peak, and adds yet another tourist attraction to Vancouver Island, already a visual delight. It is in harmony with nature (witness the restrained clearing and earthmoving, along with 12 ponds and acres of wildflowers), yet is in championship condition. Most holes feature five sets of tees, which allow a variation from 6,475 yards from the back tees to 5,185 yards from the forward blocks.

While it's called Olympic View, players also have vistas of the harbor city of Victoria and the Strait of Juan de Fuca in addition to the imposing Olympic Mountains. Golf director Earl Davies rhapsodizes about the course at every opportunity, specifically the 13th, a double-dogleg par 5 which stretches almost 600 yards to a narrow green guarded by bunkers and water. The blue tee is about 80 feet higher than the white tee.

"All you see from that tee are the mountains and a bit of the fairway," Davies says. You take a cart path up to a big rock bluff and you're actually hitting above the trees that line both sides of the fairway. You hit driver to the first corner, trying to favor the right-centre portion of the fairway, so you can fade your second shot to within 100 yards of the green. If you go left off the tee, you are blocked by an outcropping of mountain, rock and trees. There's a lake all the way down the right side of the elevated, two-tiered green which is about 175 feet deep.

While Olympic View has been tested by professionals in its infancy — pros who played in the B.C. PGA Championship called it beautiful but unforgiving – Davies foresees greater challenges.

"This course would be ideal for major tournaments," he says. "Every hole has a spot where you can sit up on the rocks and view it — almost like having a stadium course without building one. I've played a lot of golf courses and this is second to none. In my estimation, this is the most exciting golf course I've ever seen."

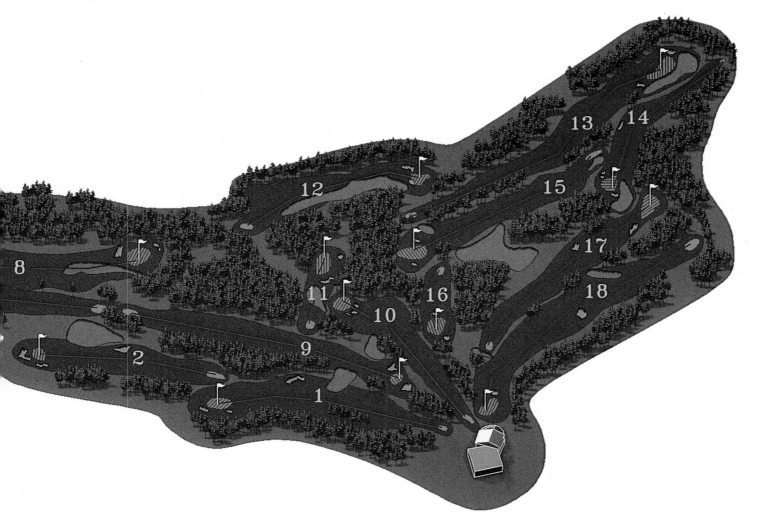

The Signature Hole at Olympic View

Head pro Doug Mahovlic calls the spectacular 17th Olympic View's signature hole. "It's the one we use on our brochures. If there are weddings here, it's the spot everyone wants to go to take pictures in front of the big waterfall. It's 417 yards from the blue tees, but it's downhill and plays shorter. With a real good tee shot, you can hit a wedge into the green.Most average golfers lay up short of a gap in the fairway 150 yards from the green. There's a bunker on the left and water for the first 200 yards on the left that doesn't come into play unless you hit a snap hook. The fairway narrows to about 30 paces at this gap because the mountain again comes into play. You hit your second shot downhill into the face of the waterfall into a green that slopes away on the left to the water. It's probably the most spectacular shot you'll see in golf today. There's a bank on the righthand side, so if you're left off the tee, you can bounce off the bank and onto the green. If you favor the right side on this hole, you can make a birdie."

Number 2 is a gambler's par 4 that dares you to use your driver.

A very impressive 20,000-square-foot club-house presides over the first and 10th tees, its rounded glass face providing another opportunity for visitors to revel in the scenery. Functionally and aesthetically pleasing, it is capable of handing groups of up to 200 for golf and/or dinner. "The design of the building, and what it does for the golfer, is so good that it could be patented," says general manager Bill Lang.

Year-round play is guaranteed by Victoria's extremely moderate climate and the 10,000 truckloads of sand and gravel placed on Olympic View's tees, greens and fairways to ensure superb drainage.

"We want to make this finest resort golf course in Canada," summarizes Davies. "A few years down the road, Olympic View could be right up there with Butchart Gardens and the Empress Hotel on the list of must-see attractions around Victoria." Lofty aims, perhaps, but one visit to Olympic View tells you those aims are not without a solid foundation.

Davies provides one example: "There I was driving around with some guests, doing my best to point out how great the golf course is, when suddenly this old fellow from Louisiana came driving by in his cart and started shaking my hand, saying it's the best damn course he's ever played. I swear it looked like we had set it up, but that's the kind of comment we hear every day."

The short but tricky par-4 12th hole at Olympic View.

PREDATOR RIDGE

Golf Resort

Architect: Les Furber
Head Professional: Sandy Kurceba
General Manager: Barrie Wheeler
Superintendent: Jim Barker

Predator Ridge Golf Resort is about a 15-minute drive south of Vernon in British Columbia's picturesque Okanagan Valley. The exact location is called "the common-age," the common area used by the local ranchers to herd cattle from Lake Kalamalka to Lake Okanagan.

The region's high, rolling hills and serpentine valleys provide the perfect landscape for a golf course. It was in 1988 when Herb and Dave Patterson of Toronto first viewed the site. The Patterson family, prominent members of the Canadian golf industry since the 1950's as the distributor for Titleist golf equipment, were aware of the rapid growth in golf and saw an opportunity to establish a world-class golf facility in the B.C. Interior.

"We knew there was growth in the area because a great barometer for golf is the sale of golf balls," says co-owner Barrie Wheeler, who formerly worked with the Patersons. "Herb had built St. Andrews East (described in the Ontario section of this book) and St. Andrews Valley and I told him, 'Don't forget your old friend when you build a third.'

"I was very impressed when I saw the area and I knew Herb would do a great job. So we bought it in 1989, and we knew it was an exceptional piece of property, ideally suited for a golf course."

Predator Ridge got its name from the lynx, bobcats and coyotes that roam its forests, but an unwary golfer can get eaten alive by the layout which calls for precise shotmaking. Architect Les Furber of Canmore, Alberta, worked on the design which will eventually comprise 36 holes.

"We knew that Les Furber had been with Robert Trent Jones for 14 years and was one of Jone's key men," recalls Wheeler. "So we knew quite a bit about Les Furber's work and that he built courses in a very similar style to those of Trent Jones. We're very pleased with the job he did here."

Furber, who has developed into one of Canada's best known course architects, utilized the natural roll of the terrain, the rocks, bluffs and lakes in designing the course, the end result being a facility that fits well with the local environment and enhances the surrounding landscape. The design philosophy developed with the owners was to intigrate the course into the convoluted terrain. "We walked the terrain with Les a lot," says Wheeler, "and agreed to work with the terrain rather than fight it."

One of the more unique features of Predator Ridge that Furber built into the design are the bentgrass target landing areas in the fairways. Wheeler thinks this course is the first in Canada to use the technique.

"Of course, now that I've said it's the first, I'll probably get calls from another course that has it, but it's very rare. It defines the landing area and gives you a beautiful target to aim at."

In addition to the brilliant green target areas, the course boasts silica bunker sand and "probably one of the largest irrigation systems ever installed," Wheeler adds. "We have 1,250 sprinklers and nearly 250 kilometres of underground piping and wire which is absolutely essential here."

The existing 18 holes are a composite of holes from the eventual 36-hole layout. Eventually, one course will remain public while the other will be exclusively for member play. "We had 30,000 rounds this year and when we hit 40,000 rounds we may complete another nine," says Wheeler, "and then we will add another nine to take it up to 36."

Plans include an expanded clubhouse for 1993 and possibly a residential development, Wheeler adds. "We've tried to have something different here at Predator Ridge, with

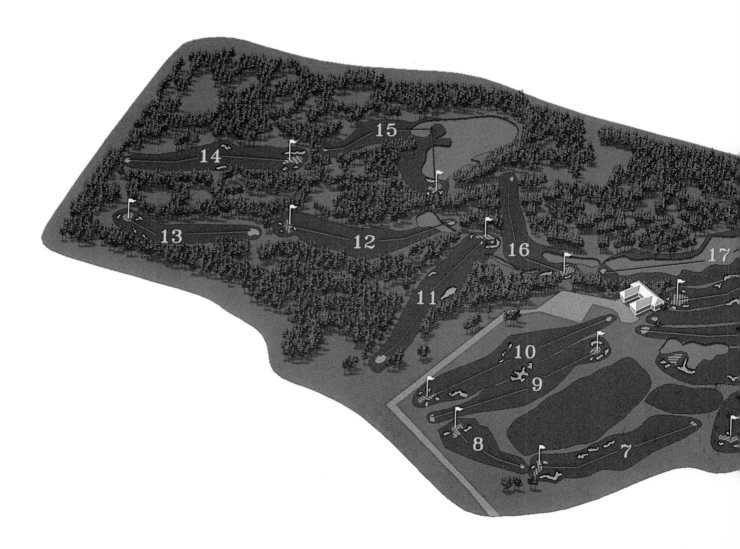

At 460 yards, the 15th is the longest par 4 at Predator Ridge.

Predator Ridge Golf Resort
Vernon, British Columbia

	Length	Par	Rating
Black	7156	73	76
Blue	6632	73	74
white	5958	73	71
Green	5475	73	68

Hole	Yards	Par			
1	418	4	10	546	5
2	347	4	11	481	4
3	166	3	12	160	3
4	568	5	13	368	4
5	223	3	14	510	5
6	401	4	15	460	4
7	408	4	16	571	5
8	195	3	17	369	4
9	521	5	18	444	4
OUT	3247	35	IN	3909	38
			Total	7156	73

The tee shot on 12 must carry a lake to reach the well-protected green.

valet parking, lessons and good people on staff. People seem to enjoy coming here to golf."

Head pro Sandy Kurceba is reticent to identify the toughest hole on the course, maintaining that each has its own character and challenge. "Number 7 is the toughest according to the scorecard, but Number 4 is probably the toughest to play."

The feared fourth is a par 5 with everything, the pro boasts. It's got sand, water, out of bounds and a large kidney-shaped green. It also has a double carry over water. The situation of the tee forces the average golfer to drive over a large pond. Those who lack nerve can aim for one of the closer landing areas and then work their way to the green.

The seventh also features a dogleg. The second shot will make or break your score on this hole. Take an extra club because you must fly the ball all the way over a gully at the front of the shallow green. "You have to get the ball airborne," says Kurceba, "you can't run it in."

Kurceba itemizes each hole, pointing out the intricacies of Furber's design. "Number 13, nicknamed Duffer's Delight, is probably the easiest to score on. It allows for a downhill tee shot to a wide-open, flat landing area." But, as with every hole at Predator Ridge, there is a catch. "The second shot is across a water hazard to a five-tiered green which is well protected by water."

Predator Ridge tested the mettle of the Canadian Tour's best players in the 1993 Xerox B.C. Open, a tribute to the calibre of such a new course.

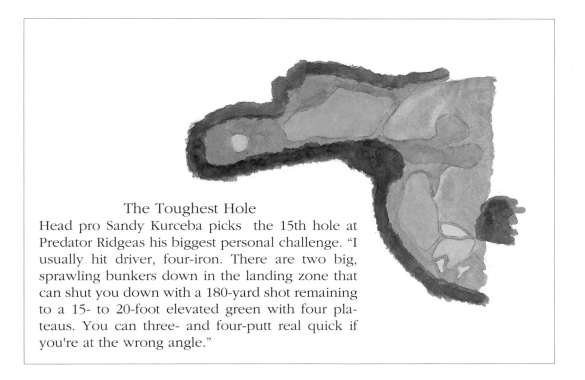

The Toughest Hole

Head pro Sandy Kurceba picks the 15th hole at Predator Ridgeas his biggest personal challenge. "I usually hit driver, four-iron. There are two big, sprawling bunkers down in the landing zone that can shut you down with a 180-yard shot remaining to a 15- to 20-foot elevated green with four plateaus. You can three- and four-putt real quick if you're at the wrong angle."

At 223 yards from the back tee, the 5th hole at Predator Ridge is a strong par 3.

—————— *Victoria, British Columbia* ——————

VICTORIA

Golf Club

Architect: A. V. Macan
Head Professional: Mike Parker
Manager: Don Francis
Superintendent: Alec Kazai

If you've heard rumors of a fantastic, mysterious golf links on Vancouver Island called Oak Bay, this is it. It has been officially known as the Victoria Golf Club since 1893, the year a band of hardy hackers rented farmland surrounded on two sides by the ocean and proceeded to lay out 11 holes. The club is the oldest in the Pacific Northwest still in existence, followed by the Tacoma Club (1894) in the neighboring state of Washington.

In his book, A Guide to the Golf Courses of British Columbia, Alan Dawe says, "Tradition has it that members of the Victoria Golf Club eventually had to buy this property because the farmers they leased it from had the unfortunate habit of driving all golfers off the fairways during the summer months so that their cows and sheep could safely graze."

If true, then that was the last time that anyone or anything forced the membership off

its links. Fiercely proud of its reputation as "the" golf club on Vancouver Island, this very private establishment is equally proud of its course — and justifiably so.

However, says Head Professional Mike Parker, if anything could push a golfer off this layout, it would be the wind. "You're right on the ocean and the wind is very much a factor," says Parker. The back tee for the par-three ninth hole is on a postage-stamp of land leaning into the ocean and new members are baptized by the spray crashing over the tee. "Sometimes you have to have someone hold your ball on the tee," says the pro, "otherwise it will blow off. Timing is very important on this shot!" On the preceding hole, a 115-yarder, Parker has hit a wedge on still days — and a hard three-iron when faced with a winter gale. Facing a winter gale is not unusual at the Victoria Golf Club. Parker says the course is open more days than any other in Canada, due to the moderate climate of southern Vancouver Island which allows golfing year-round.

Those foolish enough to write off this course as a pushover because the card reveals a length from the back tees of just over 6,000 yards are in for a rude awakening. Since positioning is vital on this narrow, devious design routed through just 97 rolling acres, it may be wise to give the driver a day off. Irons from the tee are the rule here with only a few exceptions, a situation that makes the golf course seem longer. In addition, a modern irrigation system tends to prevent any significant roll. "In large part," says Parker, "the irrigation has taken away a lot of the bump-and-run aspect of this course. Now players can fly the ball into the greens and they will hold the shot. I know players who say they used to drive the 18th

At only 145 yards, the second hole rates the nickname "Calamity."

Victoria Golf Club
Victoria, British Columbia

	Length	Par	Rating
Blue	6015	70	69
White	5857	71	68

Hole	Yards	Par
1	502	5
2	145	3
3	402	4
4	362	4
5	324	4
6	341	4
7	369	4
8	115	3
9	194	3
OUT	2754	34
10	350	4
11	438	5
12	521	5
13	158	3
14	194	3
15	404	4
16	356	4
17	450	5
18	390	4
IN	3261	37
Total	6015	71

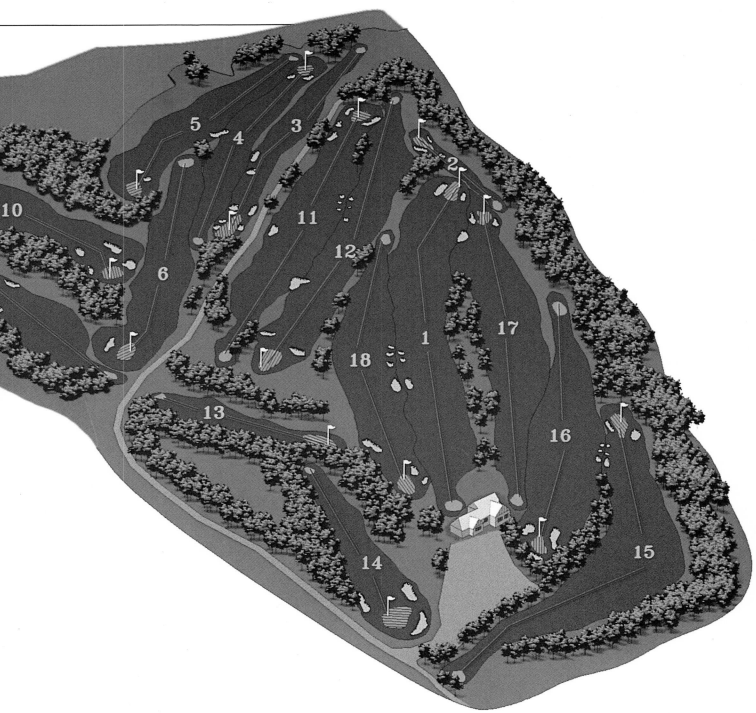

green (390 yards) in the days before irrigation, when the fairways were hard and fast. Now if you're within a hundred yards of the green, you're a hero."

Parker says the first two holes at Victoria Golf Club are reasonable warm-ups, even though the first hole is a 500-yard par-five into that notorious wind. The third hole is rated the toughest on the course and a hint of what's to come is found in its name: the Road Hole. Like its excruciatingly difficult namesake at the Old Course at St. Andrews in Scotland, a roadway figures in the layout.

But in this case, the road is Beach Drive, which trails along the left boundary of the hole. The fairway is not wide, but downwind, fortunately. Use a driver or three-wood off the tee and you will be left with a mid-iron into a three-level green that is 40 yards deep. Obviously, there is some anxiety involved in club selection for that second shot.

Once on the green, there is still much work to be done, for Victoria is touted to have the fastest greens in the West. In general, they are not large, although they do vary in size. They are characterized by undulations that are

Hole #11: 438 yards par 4

The Toughest Hole at Victoria

Though it's rated the Number 2 stroke hole, Head Professional Mike Parker calls the 11th hole at the Victoria Golf Club the most difficult on the course. It's a 438-yard par-four from the blue tees (a 458-yard par-five from the whites) and epitomizes the course's emphasis on positioning and pinpoint accuracy. "You have to play this into the wind and there's out-of-bounds all down the left side. Take a long-iron off the tee and you've still got a very difficult second shot. If you hit two good ones, you deserve to make par, and the green reflects that because it's one of the most level surfaces on the golf course."

Victoria's seaside setting contributes to its "links" atmosphere.

No. 5 is a short but exquisitely beautiful par-four.

reminiscent of the waves crashing into the nearby shore. Instead of swales, tiers and humps, one thinks of the greens as possessing breakers, combers, rollers and chutes; the putting surfaces are that idiosyncratic. "There are very few flat lies," confirms Parker. "We find it compensates for the length." Without a doubt.

The fifth hole, appropriately called The Bay, is a shortish par-four notable for two things: a very quick green even by Victoria Golf Club standards, and the start of a spectacular stretch of holes parallel to the ocean. The next hole, Vimy Ridge, forces the player to hit a blind tee shot over the ridge onto a plateau. From there, he must hit another blind shot to a green some 10 metres below the level of the fairway. "A members' hole," concedes Parker.

If you don't feel up to playing the seventh hole as a par-four, you have the option of playing it as the par-three it used to be, thanks to some novel course renovations several years ago. The ocean comes into play on the left from the tee all the way to a very severe green.

The back nine provides no respite. Hit a one- or two-iron off the tee of the 350-yard 10th hole and, if you can battle the left-to-right sloping fairway and the wind which pushes the ball right, then you will have anything from a six-iron to a wedge in. Number 12 is the first of two par-fives on the back nine. The three-level green is severely trapped with pot bunkers and mounding, making it advisable to lay up on the second shot and try to knock your third tight to the pin position of the day.

The 13th and 14th holes are par-threes, but the latter is superior, especially from the back tee which is elevated. You have no option but to hit to the green that slopes away from you — there is no fairway, and out-of-bounds lurks left, right and over the green. Your trials continue until the 17th, which Parker admits is a "members' par-five." A birdie opportunity is treasured at Victoria.

*The par-5 sixth hole at Niakwa is
reachable in two shots for long hitters.*

NIAKWA

Country Club

*Architect: Stanley Thompson
Head Professional: John Irwin
General Manager: Rick Pinchin
Superintendent: Jim Barr*

Niakwa Country Club could be the best $100,000 investment ever made in Manitoba. That is what it cost to build this time-tested layout designed by the incomparable Canadian architect Stanley Thompson. It may be hard to comprehend in the 1990s when a single membership in one of the new equity clubs may cost half that amount.

When Niakwa (the Indian word for "winding river") opened in 1923, there were 200 male shareholders who paid an annual fee of $75 and 100 ladies who contributed $100 each. The initial annual operating budget was $20,000.

The original Thompson prospectus for the course shows a layout that was never developed. This plan situated the clubhouse in the middle of the property, an unwieldy location which would have proved difficult to reach by road. Thus, Thompson reworked the drawings, except for three holes that make up Niakwa's famed "Horn," which is located near the river and has formed the hub of the layout ever since. These three signature holes are without a doubt the prettiest at Niakwa.

Thompson's final layout utilized tree-lined fairways and natural gullies to give relief from the surrounding prairie. The aforementioned small budget did not provide funds for extensive maintenance and

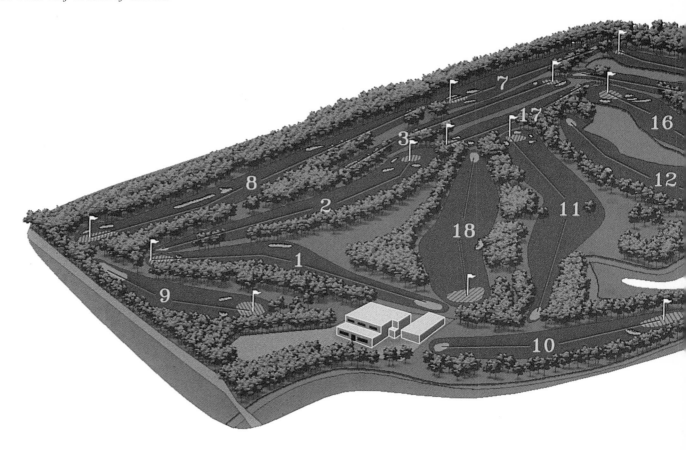

the resulting roughs made for high scores. The 1946 Canadian PGA Championship, won by Quebec's Jules Huot, attracted many U.S. PGA Tour pros, including Ben Hogan. Only five players broke par and there were only 15 rounds under 70. After the Second World War, an increased operating budget and a desire by the members to tame the course resulted in shorter rough and lower scores to the relief of all.

Like most courses, Niakwa has evolved from the original design. The current clubhouse, Niakwa's third, was constructed in 1990. The first had been situated near the 10th tee and was used from 1923 to 1950. Its demise came as a result of the Red River flood. There was a battle between the purists at the club who wanted to build on the old site and another faction of members who wanted a more spacious clubhouse with expanded facilities. The purists lost.

A new clubhouse was built on what was the old eighth hole, necessitating a revamping of Niakwa's layout. For example, a par 4 (now Number 5) was inserted between the original fourth and fifth holes. And again, when the present clubhouse was built slightly west of the second site, the members wiped out the par-3 ninth hole and changed it

again. In 1985, a new watering system was installed, causing the construction of two lakes near holes four and six. This altered those holes and the fill from the lakes was used to enhance other holes.

Niakwa, only four kilometres from the famous intersection of Portage and Main, also played host to the Canadian Open in 1961 which was won by Jackie Cupit of Texas (see sidebar). Many other significant national tournaments have been played here, including CPGA Championships in 1946, '52 and '60; the 1956 and 1972 Canadian Ladies' Amateurs, both won by the astounding Marlene Stewart Streit of Ontario; the 1974 Canadian Amateur Championship, won by Vancouver's Doug Roxburgh, who would eventually win four Amateurs; the CPGA Club Pro Championship in 1980 (Jim Collins) and 1987 (Gar Hamilton); and the Canadian Club Champions Championship, won in 1989 by Alberta's Gordon Courage.

Whether competing in a national event or simply playing a friendly game, going around Niakwa's Horn in even par is every player's dream. Due to course renovations, this quirky group of three holes is not continuous, but is made up of holes 12, 13 and 15. These three are almost all that

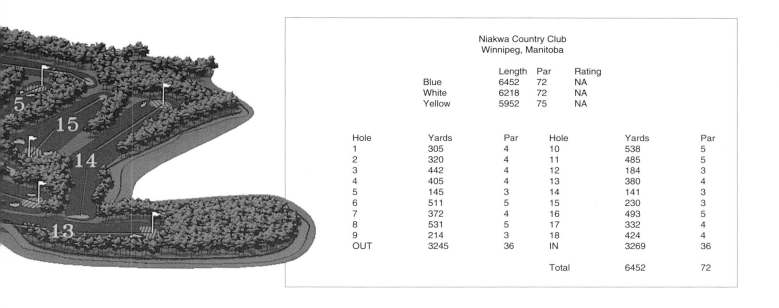

Niakwa Country Club
Winnipeg, Manitoba

	Length	Par	Rating
Blue	6452	72	NA
White	6218	72	NA
Yellow	5952	75	NA

Hole	Yards	Par	Hole	Yards	Par
1	305	4	10	538	5
2	320	4	11	485	5
3	442	4	12	184	3
4	405	4	13	380	4
5	145	3	14	141	3
6	511	5	15	230	3
7	372	4	16	493	5
8	531	5	17	332	4
9	214	3	18	424	4
OUT	3245	36	IN	3269	36
			Total	6452	72

Niakwa's famed "Horn" concludes with this diabolically difficult par 3.

remains of Stanley Thompson's original design.

The 184-yard par-3 12th, Niakwa's signature hole, marks the beginning of the Horn. From an elevated tee, the ball crosses a double bend in the Seine River, hampered by overhanging trees on the left, and an uphill apron to a tilted green, all sloped right into a full-length deep bunker.

The 13th, not a long par 4 at 380 yards, is Niakwa's most famous hole. Dubbed "an all-American hole" by Ben Hogan, the narrow fairway snakes between trees on the left and the river on the right. The second shot is uphill from a gully to the most deceptive green on the course. Many players hit close to the flagstick only to see the ball roll a good distance away. Canadian golf legend Moe Norman once hit two balls into the river here and made a nine.

The Horn concludes with a 230-yard par 3 — the toughest hole at Niakwa. From an elevated tee, you must try to hit a dramatically sloped green. The tee shot is threatened by a huge overhanging tree on the right of the green. If you play away from the tree, you must contend with bunkers on the right. Sam Snead scored one of the few holes in one ever made here during the 1946 CPGA Championship.

"Like Amen Corner at Augusta, the Horn at Niakwa deserves the same reputation as a difficult, decisive stretch of holes for determining the final score," explains long-time member Gordon Wainwright. "Over the years Niakwa has been host for many national championships, with leading men and women, amateurs and professionals — very few have escaped from the Horn unscathed."

A relatively easy par 4, the 14th is a new hole at Niakwa.

Niakwa's most famous hole, the 13th is a tremendous challenge.

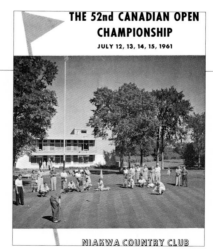

THE 52nd CANADIAN OPEN
CHAMPIONSHIP
JULY 12, 13, 14, 15, 1961

NIAKWA COUNTRY CLUB

The Umbrella Open

Gordon Wainwright, who was president of Niakwa when the 1961 Canadian Open was played there, recalls why it will be remembered as the Umbrella Open: "Many of the leading U.S. money winners, including Tony Lema, Billy Casper, Bob Goalby and Jim Ferree, came up for the Open. The weather had been excellent for weeks and the course was immaculate. Just prior to the first competitor teeing off, the rain started, and it poured and poured and poured. The rain continued for the entire four days of the Open, and that manicured layout was all but flooded. No wonder the press dubbed it the Umbrella Open. As Jacky Cupit came forward to claim the trophy, the rains ceased! And it did not rain again for weeks. The summer was dry — except for those four days in July!"

Club selection is paramount on Algonquin's par-3 third hole.

THE ALGONQUIN

Golf Course

Architect: Donald Ross
Head Professional: Lindon Garron
General Manager: Jim Frise
Superintendent: Leon Harvey

So prominent is the reputation of the stately Algonquin Resort that many people do not realize that its terra-cotta turrets and gables are part of a spectacular horizon over the tree tops along many of the 27 fine golf holes.

Built in 1889, the hotel has expanded recently, adding a 15,000-square-foot convention centre and 50 new guest rooms and suites. The tradition-laden Algonquin — renowned for its hospitality, cuisine, accommodations and healthy climate — has been enjoyed by generations of guests who visit for fun-filled vacations or memorable conferences. The year it opened, the local newspaper proclaimed in words that ring as true today: "To the summer visitors, a hearty welcome! Let their stay be short or long, let them come in the fifties or the thousands, the welcome which awaits them will be nonetheless cordial."

The tradition of the golf course parallels — indeed precedes — that of the resort itself. In 1890, the hotel owners constructed six holes in front of the hotel. In 1894, the painter, Sir William Hope, and Mr. Allen, a civil engineer from Montreal, joined up with the St. Andrews Land Co. to build nine holes behind the hotel. History will congratulate them for their foresight in hiring

Optimistic players will try to drive the 16th, a short par 4.

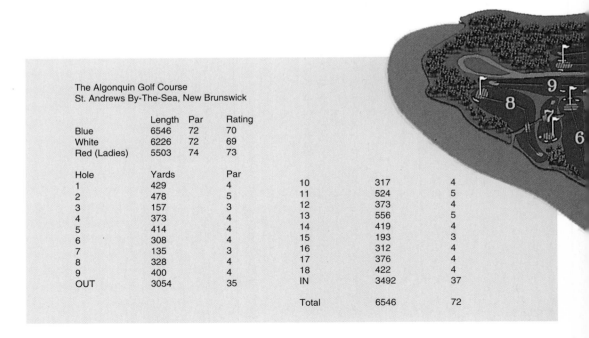

The Algonquin Golf Course
St. Andrews By-The-Sea, New Brunswick

	Length	Par	Rating
Blue	6546	72	70
White	6226	72	69
Red (Ladies)	5503	74	73

Hole	Yards	Par			
1	429	4	10	317	4
2	478	5	11	524	5
3	157	3	12	373	4
4	373	4	13	556	5
5	414	4	14	419	4
6	308	4	15	193	3
7	135	3	16	312	4
8	328	4	17	376	4
9	400	4	18	422	4
OUT	3054	35	IN	3492	37
			Total	6546	72

the revered architect Donald Ross to lay out these holes which were situated where the present holes 4 through 12 are located.

In 1900, they purchased land to construct nine more holes, which lay where 2, 3, 14, 15, 16 and 17 are now. These were laid out from Donald Ross plans by John Peacock, who became the first club manager and head professional.

A few years later, Canadian Pacific (led by T.G. Shaughnessy, who was to lend his name to a notable golf course in Vancouver) purchased the holdings of the St. Andrews Land Co., specifically the hotel and golf course. In 1916, the owners decided to lengthen the course and purchased the Poor House Farm. It is on this land that today's first and 18th holes are located.

On what remained of the Poor House Farm property, a 2,025-yard, nine-hole course was built in 1921-22. It features narrow fairways and small greens.

While anyone, no matter what their recreational preference, is guaranteed the vacation of a lifetime in the Algonquin Resort, head pro Lindon Garron says the 18-hole Seaside Course will provide all golfers with shotmaking challenges. The course also de-livers breathtaking vistas since 13 holes are played on the banks of Passamaquoddy Bay, the arm of the sea which surrounds St. Andrews.

The first hole, a 429-yard par 4, plays long into prevailing winds. A row of trees on the right extends into the fairway about 250 yards out, making an approach tough from that side. Your second shot is blind. "Very seldom can anyone hit it far enough to see the flag," says Garron. The downhill second shot requires a wood to a flat green.

The 478-yard second hole "has been described as the most difficult hole," says Garron, "but if you guard against going out of bounds on the left, especially near the green where it narrows, it's a very easy par 5." The right side of the fairway slopes into the trees and trouble.

Hitting a long iron over water can cause the faint of heart some palpitations on the 189-yard, par-3 third. Take enough club to clear the hazard, but not too much, since more trouble lurks in the bunkers behind the green. The fourth hole is aptly numbered since its near-impossible green often leads to four putts. And the fifth hole holds a special place in Garron's heart (see sidebar).

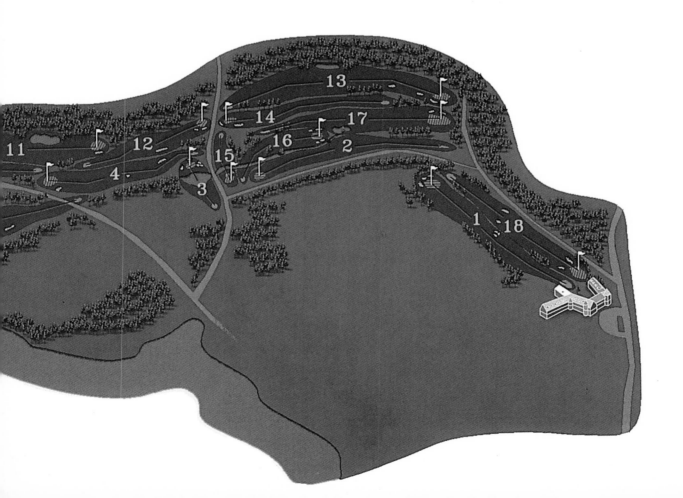

On Number 6, it is extremely easy to drive the ball into the ditch on the left. The second shot is to a tricky elevated green. On seven, says Garron, "the shot you make here is the reverse of the second shot you make on six. Here you are hitting downhill and the wind really affects the ball because you hit it so high."

The toughest part about the eighth hole is the second shot, the pro says. "It's usually a short shot, but the green slopes right to left and falls away from the golfer, so everything tends to run off the green." The front nine concludes with a 400-yard par 4 with a rise that starts at the landing area so even big hitters have a long approach shot.

The 10th is a short par 4 that compensates for its 317-yard length with a undulating, narrow, sloping green. The driver comes out of the bag on 11, a 524-yard par 5 that requires three shots for most players. On 12, Garron observes that "most drives will end up in the gully and leave you with

The Pro's Favorite

"Number 5 is one of my favorites," says Algonquin head professional Lindon Garron of this 414-yard par 4. "You get a fantastic view on both shots. When you hit off the tee, you, you're looking across the entrance of the St. Croix River and into Maine, and when you hit your second shot, you're looking out into Passamaquoddy Bay. It's much more difficult from the blue tees because you can barely get it to the corner of the sharp dogleg. The fairway starts to slope to the left at about the landing area. So, if you were to hit two similar drives, one hit down the left centre could be 40 to 50 yards farther than a ball hit to right centre. So it is possible to roll a ball around the corner."

an uphill blind second shot. The bunkers in front of the green are very deep."

On 13, the No. 1 rated hole at Algonquin, three shots are again required for all but the longest hitters. Out of bounds threatens all along the left side, and a clump of trees on the right must be avoided off the drive. Garron says 14 is one of the easiest holes on the course although plans call for the tee to be moved back to lengthen the hole to about 400 yards.

Fifteen is a good downhill par 3, where you can see the flagstick but not the green from the tee. Anything hit to the right side of the green will run into the pond. And on the 312-yard 16th, the long-hitting gambler will try to drive the green over the trees. It all depends where you stand against par at this point. Number 17 presents another blind shot where you can see the pin but not the surface of the long and narrow green. A shot

missed to the left or right drops off, making for a tough chip and putt for par.

"Number 18 is the most difficult hole on the golf course," says Garron. "The fairway is fairly wide, but you're driving uphill and there's out of bounds all the way down the left side. Your first 210 yards are uphill so if you don't hit a good drive, you're hitting into the hill. You immediately start to think about guarding your last drive of the day from going out of bounds, while knowing you have to hit it a long way to be able to get home in two shots. It's about the same length as Number 1, but the wind always seems to be against you."

With some skill and luck, you will card a 5 on Number 18 and then make your way back to the clubhouse or the hotel where a pint and a lobster dinner will put the finishing touches on another splendid day at one of Canada's finest golf resorts.

If you avoid the ditch on the left of Number 6, you still have to face a critical second shot.

Avoid the two ponds on the first hole at Granite Springs.

GRANITE SPRINGS

Golf Club

Architect: Cornish and Robinson
Head Professional: Blair Clarke
General Manager: Paul Corcoran
Superintendent: Derek Hope

The advertisement for Granite Springs Golf Club calls the course "an effort in which no compromises have been made, no corners cut." This statement is proof of truth in advertising, as is the name: there are granite outcroppings almost everywhere, and the course boasts 42 spring-fed ponds on its forested acres.

Aside from the two-storey cedar clubhouse where the motto is "the member is king," the strength of this Cornish and Robinson layout between Halifax and Peggy's Cove immediately places it among the upper echelon of Canadian courses. Bentgrass tees and greens, separated by Kentucky bluegrass fairways dotted with bunkers filled with glistening silica sand, combine with the abundance of water which will impress any golfer.

Owned by King Valley Development Corp., which also claims the equally impressive King Valley Golf Club in Ontario among its holdings, Granite Springs opened in 1991, offering non-equity transferable memberships. Under this plan, the member may sell, lease or will his or her membership at any time. This is in contrast to the traditional membership plan where the initiation fee is lost when the member leaves the club for whatever reason.

Granite Springs will cap its membership at about 500 to ensure it retains its "club" atmosphere.

"We have an interesting situation here where we do not differentiate between the ladies and the men," says manager Paul Corcoran. "The fee structure and playing privileges are the same.

"We make no pretense of the fact that we are looking to be an upscale operation, a golf club that is going to be a credit to the Halifax area. We are attracting individuals who are looking for a quality club, a club that is going to look after their personal and business needs. The clubhouse is geared to that type of operation. It is not enormous and we can't have large parties, so we will be catering to the needs of our members. However, the dining will be quite special."

The course is quite special, as well. The starting hole is a short par 5, a slight dogleg left which culminates at a green nestled among four mounds and two partially hidden ponds on the right. The second is an intriguing par 4 from both a strategic and aesthetic viewpoint: jagged white granite runs the length of the right side of the fairway, and another rock hazard faces the slightly elevated green. A long-iron tee shot should be played to the left side to avoid the water on the right.

Number 3 is a medium-length par 4 characterized by a large boulder at the back of the green. On Number 4, the long hitter must be sure to clear the brook running across the fairway. The fifth hole, a 190-yard par 3, requires a very precise shot to ensure par. On Number 6, a short but tough

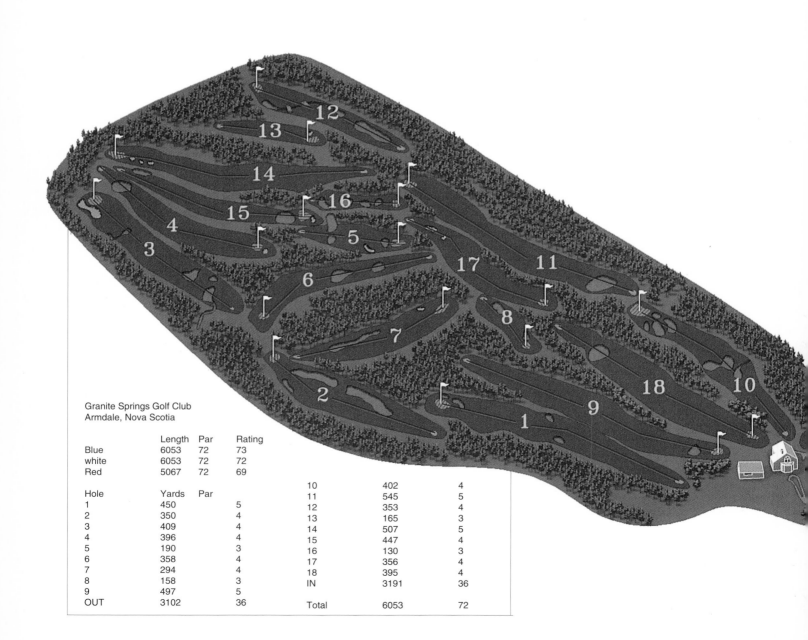

Granite Springs Golf Club
Armdale, Nova Scotia

	Length	Par	Rating
Blue	6053	72	73
white	6053	72	72
Red	5067	72	69

Hole	Yards	Par
1	450	5
2	350	4
3	409	4
4	396	4
5	190	3
6	358	4
7	294	4
8	158	3
9	497	5
OUT	3102	36

Hole	Yards	Par
10	402	4
11	545	5
12	353	4
13	165	3
14	507	5
15	447	4
16	130	3
17	356	4
18	395	4
IN	3191	36
Total	6053	72

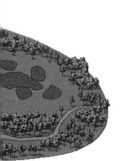

Number 12 features a three-tiered green.

par 4, the tee shot should land in the right-centre of the rolling fairway to ensure the best approach to the undulating green.

On paper, the 294-yard par-4 seventh hole is prime birdie material, but in reality a par is well earned after coping with the contoured fairway sloping upward from tee to green. The par-3 eighth hole is the number-one rated hole on the course and presents a challenge for everyone. A large rectangular water hazard extends in front of the tee, while a pond encroaches on the front and left of the green. From the tee, it appears your only play is to hit the green. The front nine concludes with a straightaway, relatively open par 5 with the requisite boulders and ponds.

While the 10th is seen as one of the most difficult holes (see sidebar), the 11th is the longest at Granite Springs. The 545-yard par 5 requires an accurate tee shot to a narrow fairway. Getting home in two is nearly impossible, due to the small size of the well-protected green. The lack of length on Number 12 is mitigated by the difficulty of the three-tiered green. Club selection is vital on the 13th, a mid-length par 3 with a green surrounded by mounds, mature oaks, birches and maples.

As you step onto the 14th tee, you are at the highest point of the course and your reward for the climb is a spectacular view — and a blind tee shot to the narrow, sloping fairway of this 507-yard par 5. The smart player will hit a long-iron just short of the three pot bunkers on the left. The 15th is a mighty par 4 at 447 yards and although the water on the left does not come into play, the two swales in the middle of the landing area do. Combine them with a brook and a sprawling pond, and you have a classic gambling hole where one could be re-warded with par — or a triple bogey.

After surviving 15, you can catch your breath on 16, the shortest hole on the course at 130 yards. Number 17 is a 356-yard dogleg-left with a boulder in the middle of the fairway. Use the large trees at the mouth of the approach shot area as targets. Approaching from the right side, there is a small, undulating green with a large rock outcropping in back. Overshooting this green could be fatal. From the elevated tee of the finishing hole, you see a pond in front of the tee as well as a large spruce in the right-centre of the fairway which makes an excellent target.

Once again, the ads for Granite Springs speak truly: "A new challenge and a new standard of service for players who expect more from the game."

The plentiful hazards on Number 8 make it a test of any golfer's skills.

The Toughest Hole at Granite Springs

The 10th hole is an exhilarating par 4 at 402 yards. From an elevated tee, one has a panoramic view of the clubhouse, driving range and countryside. There are two ponds on the right side of the fairway and another ahead and to the left. The landing area slopes gradually to the right. Approaching the green are two ponds to the right and one on the left. The golfer is then faced with a sheer rock face leading to the elevated green. In the words of Peter Hope, one of the all-time outstanding golfers in Atlantic Canada and past-president of the Royal Canadian Golf Association, the 10th "is a great hole to start the back nine, with seven clear blue ponds and a uniquely placed green presenting the player with many challenges. This hole requires an accurate three-wood or one-iron tee shot to the right-centre of the fairway, leaving an approach of roughly 150 yards. Aggressiveness on this hole could be costly."

True to its name, this course is dotted with white boulders and shimmering ponds.

Known locally as "Killer," the long and narrow seventh hole is the toughest test at Highlands Links on Cape Breton Island.

HIGHLANDS LINKS

Cape Breton Highlands National Park

Architect: Stanley Thompson
Head Professional: Joe Robinson
Superintendent: Martin Walsh

"This is the Cypress Point of Canada for sheer beauty," the late George Knudson once labelled Highlands Links. "When you're driving up the road to the course, it's like driving up to heaven."

Emerging from the fog which often enshrouds the top of Smoky Mountain, the highest point in Nova Scotia near the outermost tip of Cape Breton Island, awaits a heavenly golf experience indeed. For there, carved out of virgin forest 50 years ago, rests a rugged giant called Highlands Links.

When Stanley Thompson trekked to the wilds of Cape Breton at the invitation of the federal government, to build a course within the confines of Cape Breton Highlands National Park, he discovered a challenge appropriate for the man who constructed such wilderness gems as Banff Springs and Jasper Park.

"Stanley Thompson in his early days sometimes would use little more than instinct in laying out his courses . . . striving to retain as much of the natural ground formation as possible. The most beautiful courses, he is convinced — the ones where the greens invite your shots — are the ones which hew most closely to nature," John La Cerda wrote in the Saturday Evening Post in 1946. Highlands Links, like his glorious Capilano on Canada's western coast in West Vancouver, demonstrates the genius of Thompson's instinct.

Highlands Links Ingonish Beach, Nova Scotia				Hole	Yards	Par	Hole	Yards	Par
				1	413	4	10	151	3
				2	441	4	11	534	5
	Length	Par	Rating	3	143	3	12	227	3
Blue	6588	72	72	4	326	4	13	423	4
White	6193	71	71	5	164	3	14	411	4
Yellow	5659	76	73	6	532	5	15	548	5
				7	570	5	16	460	5
				8	314	4	17	190	3
				9	337	4	18	409	4
				OUT	3240	36	IN	3348	36
							Total	6588	72

Like all the par-threes at Highlands Links, the 10th hole is pretty, but tough.

Here, in the shadow of Mount Franey, within sight of the Atlantic Ocean and the Clyburn River, using manual labor and horsedrawn implements, Thompson created a masterpiece. It does not overpower with length (the course plays less than 6,600 yards from the tips), but rather with relentless demands on the golfer to produce the exact shot required.

Although the actual golf holes are not lengthy by modern standards, be prepared for a vigorous outing. The links-style course (nine holes out from the clubhouse and nine back) loops around an 11-kilometre routing. A walk from one green to the next tee may cover 300 metres or more, but the flora, fauna and spectacular scenery make the exertion worthwhile. Golf carts are not available. "Take a box lunch out there, go out for 18 holes and you're gone for the day," Knudson advised.

On most holes, a level lie is the only reward for a perfectly placed shot; on some, the teeing ground offers the only flat surface. During construction, huge boulders were tumbled onto the fairways, covered with topsoil and seed, and have become massive moguls to be negotiated with extreme care. The greens, as inviting as Thompson may have intended them, are characterized by swales running through the surface and flanked by sand traps.

After negotiating the first hole, a 408-yard

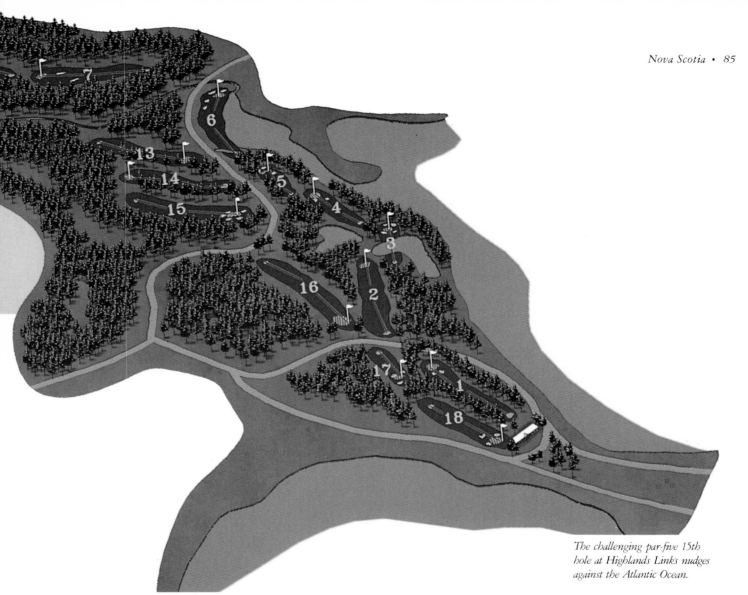

The challenging par-five 15th hole at Highlands Links nudges against the Atlantic Ocean.

par-four, you look back at the modest club-house, and beyond in stark contrast to the deep green forest covering Mount Franey, sits Keltic Lodge. With its white clapboard and red tile roof, the quaint, comfortable lodge (world-renowned for its lobster dinners) is only a few hundred metres from the course.

All the holes bear Gaelic names, as befits a course called Highlands Links. Some are humorous ("Muckle Mouth Meg"), others puzzling ("Tattie Bogle" translates as "potato pits"), but few are as appropriate as that affixed to the fourth hole: Heich O'Fash (Heap of Trouble).

Rated as the Number 1 stroke hole, the 270-yard 4th (Heich O' Fash) deceives the unwary or the over-confident player with its lack of length. An accurate tee shot will attain the top of a plateau which rises from the fairway about 150 yards out. Approach shots to the green, situated on a second plateau, must take into account the ugly fact that inaccuracy will be punished severely. Being left or right could mean a lost ball, while the cunningly sloped green may reject a less-than-perfect attempt and spit it into the trees and tangled

rough which surround the putting surface.

One of Thompson's trademarks, fairway bunkers some 30 yards short of the green, provide another unwelcome surprise on the fourth hole. First-time players may assume these bunkers are green-side and find themselves two or three clubs short on their approach. After surviving Heich O'Fash, glance right to see another emblem of Highlands Links' uniqueness: lobster dories tied up where the river juts into the adjacent fairway.

The seventh hole is called Killiecrankie, which translates as "a long and narrow pass," but perhaps the local nickname, "Killer," reveals more about its character. A 556-yard par-five, the seventh is rated the toughest hole on the course. Bounded by majestic maples, the narrow double-dogleg defends itself admirably from those long hitters who try to reach the green in two. Its defences include Highlands Links' ever-present uneven lies, and a huge bunker guarding the right side of the green. Your task is far from complete once on the

putting surface: a long, two-tiered green offers a myriad of pin locations.

On Number 15 (Tattie Bogle), the ideal tee shot requires a powerful blow over the hill on the left. The third shot on this 546-yard par-five is to a green, surrounded by five bunkers, which sits almost at the front doorstep of St. Paul's Church. First-time visitors are sometimes seen wandering through the adjacent graveyard, pulling golf carts, trying to find the 16th tee.

You may want to take a cue from some of the locals, who dip their golf balls into the holy water at St. Paul's on the way to Number 16. Aptly named Sair Fecht (Hard Work), this relatively short par-five is merciless, but a fantastic golf hole nonetheless. The opening drive on this 458-yarder must carry a ravine or it's "three from the tee." Only a slightly better fate awaits those who hit it straight, for the fairway undulations resemble the surface of the neighboring Atlantic during a winter storm. Picture a herd of buried elephants

One of the many unusual aspects of Highlands Links is the Gaelic names given to each hole. Some relate to an aspect of the hole, others were selected simply because of their colorful Scottish flavor. Photograph is of hole number 15, Tattie Bogle.

1. BEN FRANEY: Playing through this fairway presents a full view of Ben Franey. "Ben" is Scottish for "mountain."
2. TAM O'SHANTER: A Scot's bonnet is known as a Tam O'Shanter; in this case, the shape of the green is the reason for the appelation.
3. LOCHAN: A small sheet of water, or miniature lake.
4. HEICH O'FASH: Heap of trouble.
5. CANNY SLAP: A small opening, or "slap", in a hedge or fence.
6. MUCKLE MOUTH MEG: Reportedly, Muckle Mouth Meg, a Scottish lass from Hawick, could swallow a whole "Bubbly Jock's Egg" (a turkey egg).
7. KILLERCRANKIE: A long, narrow pass
8. CABER'S TOSS: The follow-through after tossing the caber (a log used during Highland games) can be described as "up and over."
9. CORBIE'S NEST: A corbie is a crow, while "nest" is high ground.
10. CUDDY'S LUGS: Donkey's ears. A description of the green.
11. BONNIE BURN: A pleasant stream.

12. CLEUGH: Cleugh is a term used for placenames in the Cheviot hills of Scotland. It means a deep gully or ravine with precipitous sides.
13. LAIRD: A Scottish land owner.
14. HAUGH: A small hollow or valley.
15. TATTIE BOGLE: Potato pits. Potatoes are placed in pits and covered with thatch.
16. SAIR FECHT: Hard work.
17. DOWIE DEN: The Scottish border ballad "The Dowie Dens of Yarrow" relates to a massacre.
18. HAME NOO: Home now.

trooping down the fairway and you have a fairly accurate idea of the lie you face.

Parks Canada has been criticized for not contributing enough money to adequately maintain this national treasure, but that situation appears to be improving. Highlands Links hired its first professionally trained course superintendent in 1990, and improve-

ments are noticeable already. This is a golf experience that, regretably, few Canadians have savored. It is guaranteed not to disappoint.

Members of other distinguished golf clubs in Atlantic Canada call Highlands Links "the best course in the world." After delighting in the wild, ethereal beauty of this unique links layout, you may be inclined to agree.

The swales and humps on the 14th hole are typical of the Stanley Thompson layout.

Picturesque and challenging. Your second shot on 18 strongly influences the outcome of this long finishing hole.

BARRIE NATIONAL PINES

Golf and Country Club

Architect: Thomas McBroom
Director of Golf: Ed Membery
Head Professional: Doug Warner
Superintendent: Chris Goodman

Barrie National Pines is somewhat like a Model T with a turbocharged engine under the hood. The overall feeling is very traditional, due in large part to the classic styling of the logo and signage, as well as to the post-and-beam construction of the unpretentious yet comfortable clubhouse.

But stepping onto the first tee, there's a rush of adrenalin as you realize that this may be one of the best courses you will ever play. And that excitement continues to accelerate throughout the round until you putt out on the 18th hole.

The brainchild of longtime CPGA pro Ed Membery, Barrie National Pines is just south of one of Canada's fastest-growing cities. Membery and his partner, Eugene Boccia, selected this 200-acre parcel of land east of Highway 400 using a number of criteria, and Lovers Creek was near the top of the list.

Lovers Creek wends its way through the property, necessitating the building of nine bridges and coming into play 14 times during a round. Membery, in collaboration with Toronto architect Tom McBroom, has produced a very private, walkable layout that not only protects the scenic creek's environmental integrity, but makes full use of it as a design consideration and hazard.

McBroom, a man with an understanding of golf beyond his

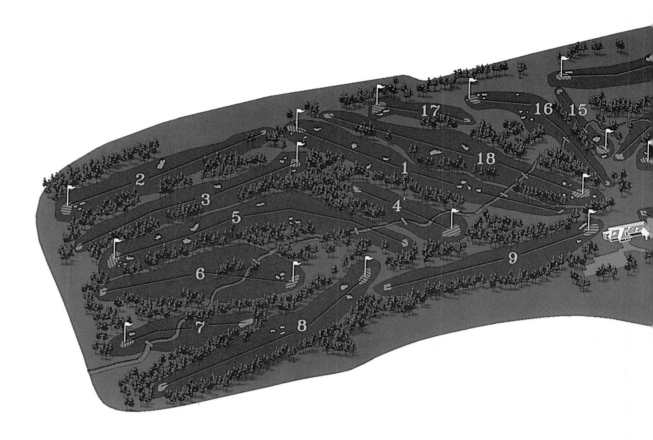

years, took full advantage of the property's intricate topography in creating this 7,000-yard masterpiece.

Nine of the 18 fairways traverse Lovers Creek. Each of the 18 unique holes offers five different tee decks, guaranteeing variety to the members as well as offering an opportunity for golfers of all abilities to complete an enjoyable round.

Upon playing the course, it becomes clear that while the stands of mature trees, the scenic vistas and the gentle rolling hills provide the inspiration; the astute placement of the water hazards, the bunkers filled with brilliant white Ohio sand, grassy hollows and thick roughs provide the challenge. An ideal summer for growing conditions in 1992 helped the accomplished greens staff in bringing Barrie National Pines to peak condition in record time.

"I would characterize Barrie National Pines as a course in the parkland style," McBroom says. "It is a strong site, mostly treed, which provided for strong definition of the fairways right off the bat. We had an immediate feeling of maturity.

"The land is gently rolling and the difficulty is created by the number and location of the trees, obviously, as well as Lovers Creek. We tried to integrate the creek in a number of different ways strategically, opening up greens from different directions and challenging the player in different ways. On Number 14, for example, we used the creek in a manner very similar to that on Number 12 at Augusta. You must hit a lofted club to a narrow green; the challenge is obviously in club selection."

Lovers Creek not only adds to the challenge of the playing the course, says McBroom, it demonstrates how, in his words, "golf course design is creatively responding to environmental concerns.

"The creek, like all wetlands and waterways, is protected by the conservation authorities which require that the fairways be set back from the water, among other requirements. You can't manicure the fairways right up to the bank. Our response, from a design perspective, was to go at the creek on the diagonal to create a 'bite off as much as you can chew' philosophy. It creates a unique

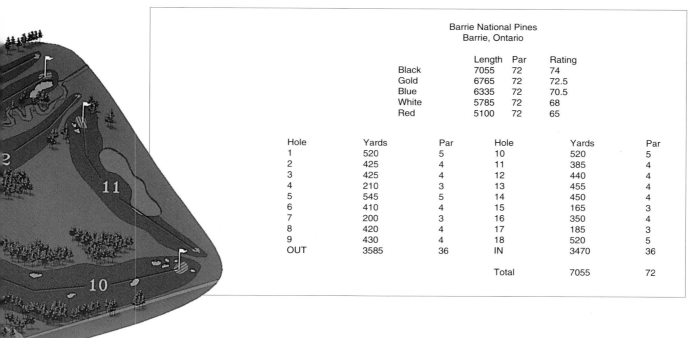

Barrie National Pines
Barrie, Ontario

	Length	Par	Rating
Black	7055	72	74
Gold	6765	72	72.5
Blue	6335	72	70.5
White	5785	72	68
Red	5100	72	65

Hole	Yards	Par	Hole	Yards	Par
1	520	5	10	520	5
2	425	4	11	385	4
3	425	4	12	440	4
4	210	3	13	455	4
5	545	5	14	450	4
6	410	4	15	165	3
7	200	3	16	350	4
8	420	4	17	185	3
9	430	4	18	520	5
OUT	3585	36	IN	3470	36
			Total	7055	72

At 350 yards the par-4 16th is the shortest on the course. Avoid the four fairway bunkers on the left.

*Slicers beware! Placement of the tee
shot on the 11th is of paramount
importance.*

challenge while at the same time protecting the creek."

Barrie National Pines is one of the new breed in other ways, as well. It is a true equity club, wherein the members own the course and all its assets. Equity memberships are transferable and assignable, subject only to the clubs' bylaws.

While the majority of members are from the Barrie area, marketing manager Brian Allen says the hour-long drive from Toronto has not deterred golfers from that city from joining. "They're willing to drive up to an hour to golf because of the lineups at courses in the To-ronto area." It also doesn't hurt that the membership fee at Barrie National Pines is about half of that at a comparable Toronto course — if you could find a comparable course!

The post-and-beam clubhouse, with hunter green accents, holds its own with the calibre of the course and it's obvious from the friendly staff that Barrie National Pines is as good to work at as it is to golf at. "We feel very strongly that the golf industry is part of the hospitality industry," Allen says. "Our priority is to ensure that our members enjoy every moment they spend here, whether it's on the course, in the clubhouse or on the range."

The Toughest Hole

Thomas McBroom, the architect who designed Barrie National Pines, picks Number 13 as the toughest hole on the course. "This hole is difficult for every player," says McBroom, a fine golfer himself. "You are faced with a strategic forced carry off the tee and then the length of the hole, which generally plays into the wind, means you'll probably be hitting a two-iron in. An easy 5, but a very difficult 4."

One of nine holes which cross Lovers Creek. The angled green requires patience and accuracy.

The 400-yard 13th hole signals the start of Beacon Hall's toughest stretch.

——— *Aurora, Ontario* ———

BEACON HALL

Golf and Country Club

Architect: Bob Cupp with Thomas McBroom
Head Professional: Phil Hardy
Manager: Gary Carl

Beacon Hall has been called "the most exclusive golf club in Canada," and it may well be in terms of number of members. A mere 230 purists belong to this classically understated refuge built on a magnificent site north of Toronto. Indeed, only a handful of golf clubs in North America have a smaller membership roster. Membership at Beacon Hall is not something one brags about, but it is something to be very proud of — the course was ranked fifth in the country by SCORE, the national golf magazine, in its first year of eligibilty in 1990.

From the back tees, Beacon Hall approaches 7,000 yards, "a course for players of supreme ability," says course architect Bob Cupp, himself a former PGA Tour pro. "Though they are few, they do have a tremendous influence over the reputation of the course." Cupp says that while the course could host any tournament from a stategic point of view, due to the underlying philosophy of the wealthy members to shun publicity, "there will be no accommodations for gallery or tournament operations. This is a course for the members — but with enough teeth to gain the respect of even the severest critics." This is not to say that Cupp's design excludes players of lesser ability: "The members' course will be

all of the members' course," he says, and it is true that the other tee postions offer a gratifying, yet challenging, test.

The very existence of Beacon Hall is gratifying as well to those few individuals who, concerned about crowded conditions at other Toronto private clubs, decided to assemble a group to purchase the former Toronto and North York Hunt Club and an adjacent farm to give Cupp the land he needed to create a "world-class" facility. As well, 80 attractive, expensive and unobtrusive housing units were planned: their sale would provide true aficionados with a residence on one of the country's finest course and assist with the project's financing. Cupp was impressed by the group's efforts, calling the 260 acres the best piece of property he had ever had the opportunity to work with. The result, which opened in 1988, is a golfer's dream: a masterful routing taking full advantage of the property's varying personalties. "Every shot will be presented like

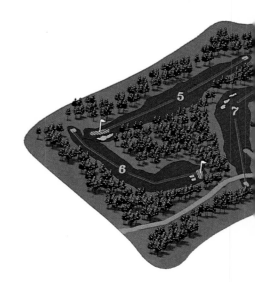

The third hole at Beacon Hall winds through pines reminiscent of the Carolinas.

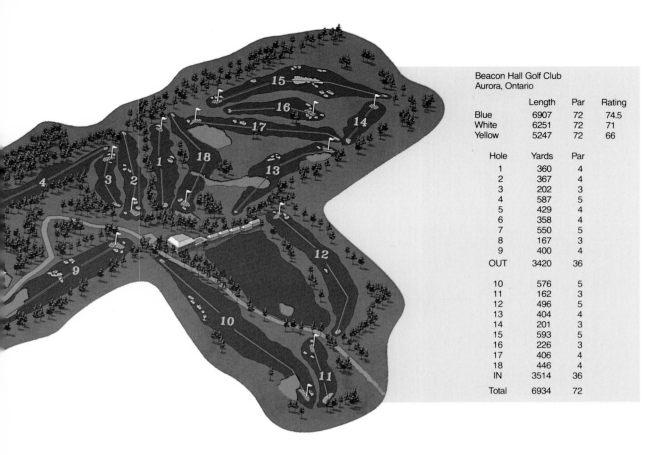

Beacon Hall Golf Club		
Aurora, Ontario		
	Length	Par	Rating
Blue	6907	72	74.5
White	6251	72	71
Yellow	5247	72	66

Hole	Yards	Par
1	360	4
2	367	4
3	202	3
4	587	5
5	429	4
6	358	4
7	550	5
8	167	3
9	400	4
OUT	3420	36
10	576	5
11	162	3
12	496	5
13	404	4
14	201	3
15	593	5
16	226	3
17	406	4
18	446	4
IN	3514	36
Total	6934	72

a picture," Cupp resolved when designing the course, and he delivered on that promise.

The first four holes play through towering red pines reminiscent of the Carolinas, and then the vegetation makes a pleasing switch to burly hardwoods — maples, oaks and walnuts. The back nine, with its mammoth sand hill and swales swathed in native grasses, takes the player on an imaginary and tactical visit to the links courses of Scotland and Ireland. The finishing hole unites the features in summary; looking back off the tee, adjacent to the first green and its protective pines, your eyes pan across the sandy mounds of the back nine, but your drive must carry uphill through more hardwoods.

"I think Bob Cupp designed the course beautifully," says Head Professional Phil Hardy. "The first six holes combine a gentle invitation to the course with a taste of what's to come. The next six say, 'Here's where you make your move,' with their three par-fives. The final six are all golf. They've killed a lot of hopes. I've seen great players come to 15, 16, 17 or 18 at- or under-par and walk off the course without finishing."

That last stretch obviously is key to a good round at Beacon Hall. It commences with Number 13, a 400-yard par-four with a generous fairway, inviting the player to "bust it," says Cupp. As on many of the holes, the fairway bunkers — on the left in this case — indicate the best postion. "At this course, the fairway bunkers are usually saying, 'Come as close to me as you dare,'" says Hardy. "They indicate where you have the best approach, where you will have the most green to work with." On 13, you are penalized if you don't flirt with these traps: an approach from anywhere else must carry over a particularly nasty greenside bunker.

The next hole plays 199 yards from the back tees. This claustrophic par-three is hemmed in on three sides by mounds or hills. The green is guarded by two bunkers, one of which is three metres deep. If you are playing the white tees, play safe to the left and bounce the ball onto the green, advises Cupp.

The par-five 15th hole presents a heroic challenge from the tee. Its split fairway is separated by a waste bunker the size of a football field — one acre in area. The short, or left, route requires precision to place the ball in a landing area only 30 yards wide, but offers

The 18th hole at Beacon Hall rises toward the clubhouse.

the successful gambler a long-iron approach to a severely contoured green guarded by three bunkers on the right. The player who elects to stay right and hope for par must follow Cupp's prescription: A drive to the corner of the dogleg, a long-iron or fairway wood near a bunker set in a mogul on the right side and then a wedge to cover the remaining 80 or 90 yards to the two-tiered green.

"If there is a supreme test at Beacon Hall, this is it," says Cupp about the par-three 16th, and everyone who has played the course agrees with him. At 228 yards from the blue tees and 213 from the whites, this hole may require more club than some players have in their bags, especially if played into the wind. The intervening area between the elevated tee and green is layered in tall, waving fescue grass

and swallows any errant shot, although there is a landing area left of the green.

The 17th hole, a straightaway par-four, reiterates one of the underlying design principles at Beacon Hall: play as close as you can to the fairway bunkers on the right because the green opens up fully from that side. Being in the left greenside bunker means playing out of the sand directly toward a pond — not a desireable scenario.

As mentioned, the finishing hole combines all the esthetic qualities of the property, but it also presents the final strategic challenge of the round. A good drive on this lengthy par-four (448 from the blues, 409 from the whites) will be followed by a long-iron toward the well-mounded and - bunkered green near the clubhouse.

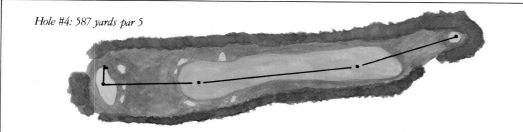

Hole #4: 587 yards par 5

The Toughest Hole at Beacon Hall

The 587-yard fourth hole, the first par-five encountered at Beacon Hall, is rated the most difficult hole on the course. In the words of course designer Bob Cupp, "The drive will be played from an elevated tee across a depression to a fairway rising and winding to the right. The tee shot from the white and yellow markers will be substantially farther forward, but uphill. Once the players successfully reaches the first landing area, the next challenge is reaching the second landing area and 'setting up' the approach. The second landing area is actually in the shape of a giant green, nearly 47,000 square feet — about an acre — and a fair challenge for the three-wood or long-iron required to get there. From anywhere on the second landing area, the green will be visible and a fair target. The shot to the green will be the first true test of the round. The putting surface lies at the top of a rise. Three bunkers rest in the front slope of the green area. The back is supported by low mounds. Anything over the green will roll down the backslope; a formidable hazard."

The greens at Beacon Hall are straightforward; the challenge is to get to them in regulation.

Number 15 demands a 240-yard carry to reach the fairway from the back tees.

BLUE SPRINGS

Golf Club

Architect: Don Dawkins
Director of Golf Operations: Craig Guthrie
Head Professional: Shelley Woolner
Superintendent: Ted Ellis

"Unique" may be an overworked term when it comes to golf courses, but it is appropriate when applied to Blue Springs Golf Club near Guelph.

Built on a 540-acre site with dramatic elevation changes, 23 ponds and stands of mature forest, Blue Springs is the brainchild of Don Dawkins, founder of the Olde Hide House. The slogan of the Olde Hide House, a retailer of leather furniture and apparel, is "it's worth the drive to Acton." Dawkins' latest venture makes that doubly true.

Dawkins and his partners have used their marketing genius to put the name of Blue Springs on many golfers' lips, nationally as well as locally. One of their first moves was to negotiate a deal with the Canadian Professional Golfers' Association to build its headquarters there. As part of the agreement, Blue Springs will play host to one of the CPGA's national championships every year. "The move made sense for us because of the good management and the outstanding golf course," says CPGA Executive Director Dave Colling.

The next move was to develop a teaching program in which head pro Shelley Woolner and Ben Kern from the National Golf

The par-5 12th yeilds may more double bogeys than birdies.

Blue Springs Golf Club
Acton, Ontario

	Length	Par	Rating
Gold	6715	72	73.5
Blue	6406	72	71.9
White	6106	72	70.4
Red	5188	72	65.8

Hole	Yards	Par
1	373	4
2	217	3
3	330	4
4	524	5
5	183	3
6	366	4
7	421	4
8	392	4
9	485	5
OUT	3291	36
10	425	4
11	156	3
12	515	5
13	384	4
14	451	4
15	512	5
16	386	4
17	177	3
18	423	4
IN	3424	36
Total	6715	72

Club offer instruction packages ranging from an hour to a week at Blue Springs' great facilites.

The membership concept combines the best of both worlds. While Blue Springs is open to the public, a small number of transferable memberships is available, offering advanced booking of tee times, unrestricted use of various facilities and virtually unlimited play on the Turtle Lake and Trillium courses. That's right — Dawkins and his group had the foresight to build not one, but two layouts.

The Turtle Lake course is a 6,700-yard test while the Trillium is a nine-hole, par-3 track ideal for beginners, juniors and seniors. "Unique" may be applied to the way they were created.

In 1987, Dawkins says, "we had an Olde Hide House management meeting and the decision was made to diversify. Golf and real estate were the first options that came up and within a year of that discussion we bought the property to develop that idea."

The final result covered both goals. In addition to the golf component, there are 40 estate lots of between one and three acres overlooking the courses.

Dawkins, the nominal architect, says everyone on the management committee, "whether their handicap was five or 35," had input into the design of the course. Hole design was continually in flux, even during the building stages, with par 3s being changed to par 4s, and so on. "Our affiliation with the CPGA meant we had to go for quality," Dawkins says. "During construction we redesigned four holes. We didn't hesitate to evaluate what we were doing while we were doing it. We did this more as a work of art than an engineering project."

While the staggering elevation changes make a cart all but a necessity, the Turtle Lake course reflects its democratic origins by offering an enjoyable experience for golfers of all skill levels. Four sets of tees mean the length of the course can vary from 6,715 yards to 5,188. Every aspect of a player's game is examined during a round here, especially putting.

Several holes merit special attention, in-

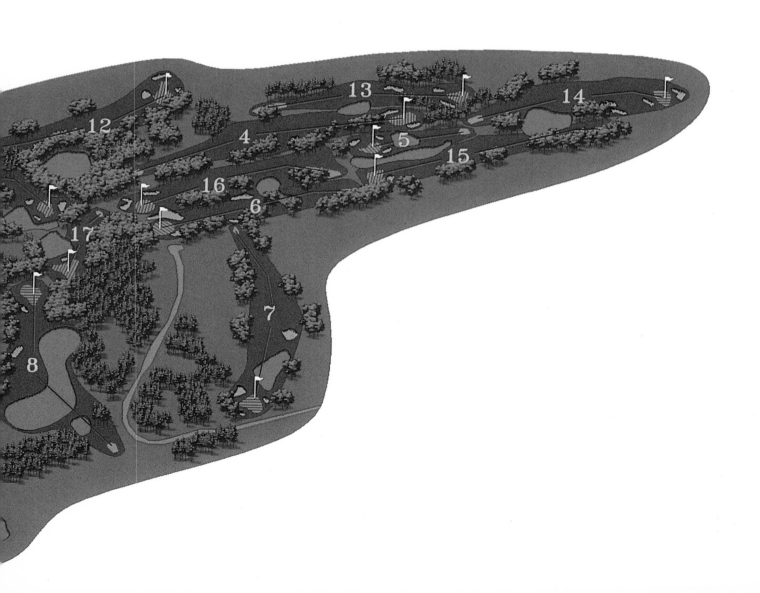

The Eighth Hole at Blue Springs

The eighth hole has been identified as one of the signature holes at Blue Springs — although the course has been called "a collection of signature holes" — and it may be the toughest. The drive originates from an elevated tee set back in a chute of trees, and it must carry a large pond to a generous landing area with a large fairway bunker. It is a classic challenge of the "risk-reward" school of design. The more you cut across the pond, the shorter your approach shot is. The second shot into an sloping, narrow green must thread the needle between woods on the right and a bunker on the front left.

Many call the 17th Blue Springs' "signature hole."

An elevated tee, water and rock make the 10th a dramatic hole.

cluding the second, eighth (see sidebar), the 10th, 14th and 17th.

The par-3 second hole stretches to 217 yards from the back tees and, if the wind is blowing, is a stern test. Adding to the difficulty is a large bunker on the front left and four pot bunkers behind. The tee is elevated with the large sloping green set in the valley below. "The hole was set up with two very difficult pin placements," say the designers. "The back right means the golfer must contend with the traps, while a back left position means using a wood off the tee."

The 10th has been called "one of the most dramatic holes at Blue Springs." A 425-yard par 4, the hole plays to a green almost 100 yards below the teeing ground. Length off the tee is not critical, but accuracy on the second shot is. An elevated green is surrounded by a pond, bunkers and bush on the back and left. The hole is visually striking, with natural rock forming a backdrop to the pond. "The back-bone of a golf course is the long par 4" say the designers, "and this is it on Blue Springs."

The 14th is a 450-yard dogleg right and the longest of the par 4s. You don't normally get a break from the wind on this hole; it's usually in your face as you stand on the tee. Five tee blocks add to the flexibility if the wind is too strong. The front tees are some 130 yards closer to the pin. A 200 foot long trap engulfs the right side of the fairway, forcing golfers to stay left, and then large traps surround the green, making an accurate long-iron shot a must. Things don't get any easier once you get to the green, which slopes from back to front."

The 17th is notable not necessarily because of its difficulty but because of its beauty. Its length varies from 177 from the golds to 136 at the forward tees, allowing every player to enjoy its attributes. Played from the top of a cliff some 80 feet above the green over a pond and small waterfall to a large sloping green framed by trees, the 17th is a memorable hole. From the championship tees, 10 holes are clearly visible.

Camelot's 16 hole is a short but challenging par 5.

Ottawa, Ontario

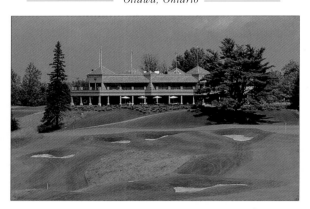

CAMELOT

Golf and Country Club

Architect: Thomas McBroom
General Manager: Don Noseworthy
Head Professional: Barry Laphen
Superintendent: Robin Stafford

"God himself put this piece of land here for a golf course," says Camelot co-founder Don Noseworthy. And it is with near-religious fervor that Noseworthy preaches the merits of this magnificent layout just east of Canada's capital city.

Obviously, Noseworthy is not alone in his lofty estimation of Camelot. In 1993, the course was selected as runnerup by the U.S. publication Golf Digest in the category "best new private course in Canada," and anyone fortunate enough to play it will not question the judges' decision which is based on the criteria of shot values, playability, design balance, memorability and aesthetics.

Overlooking the mighty Ottawa River, Camelot offers a vast variety of aesthetic and golfing pleasures. Nature did its part by providing stands of ancient pines, rippling lakes, significant elevation changes and precipitous ravines.

"It's a gorgeous site," agrees course architect Tom McBroom of Toronto. "It's half woods and half open, situated on a high ridge overlooking the Ottawa River. From the clubhouse, you can see 30 miles down the river as well as overlooking nine

holes of the golf course. It's a really dramatic property punctuated by steep wooded slopes. The site offers spectacular elevated tee shots.

"Camelot is really a combination of two characteristics. It's links-style up top in the meadowland where the holes are defined by the fescue roughs. The rest is situated in a woodsy parkland. It's a great contrast.

"I think Camelot is important in a number of ways," says the architect, "not the least of which is that it is the first significant addition to the Ottawa Valley golf scene in decades; since the opening of Royal Ottawa and Ottawa Hunt."

This "significant addition" is the realized dream of one man — Don Nose-worthy. He describes how the vision of Camelot came to him:

"I was returning from Pebble Beach following Tom Watson's dramatic victory over Jack Nicklaus in 1982 when I made the decision to build a golf course. Pebble Beach has always been my favorite place on earth and I am certain that the inspiration to fulfil a life-long dream began amid the wind and the beauty of Pebble Beach.

"The Ottawa River is not the Pacific Ocean," acknowledges the man who became Camelot's first president and general manager, "but the views from the land we chose in 1988 are spectacular.

Noseworthy says other names were considered before settling on Camelot. "Some of the interesting connections between our course and the original Camelot include the fact that King Arthur and his Knights of the Round Table were originally thought to occupy a part of England known as Cumberland. Cumberland is the name of the township where the golf course is located.

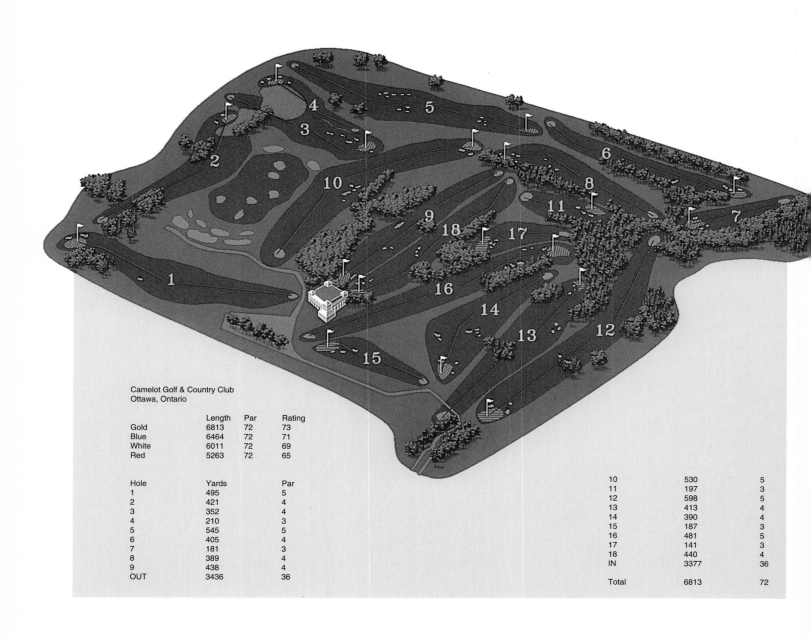

Camelot Golf & Country Club
Ottawa, Ontario

	Length	Par	Rating
Gold	6813	72	73
Blue	6464	72	71
White	6011	72	69
Red	5263	72	65

Hole	Yards	Par
1	495	5
2	421	4
3	352	4
4	210	3
5	545	5
6	405	4
7	181	3
8	389	4
9	438	4
OUT	3436	36

Hole	Yards	Par
10	530	5
11	197	3
12	598	5
13	413	4
14	390	4
15	187	3
16	481	5
17	141	3
18	440	4
IN	3377	36
Total	6813	72

Cut the dogleg on Number 14 — if you dare.

"In addition there was a huge stone on the property that was perfect for inserting Excalibur, the magic sword. And the code of ethics of the Knights of the Round Table were not unlike the ethics portion of the Rules of Golf. Besides, as the song says: 'In short, there's simply not a more congenial spot than Camelot.'"

Having found the property and selected the name, Noseworthy entered into a partnership with local businessmen Philippe and Andre Gagnon. "We decided to go the equity route to raise the funds to build our dream," recalls Noseworthy. "I sold my business and became the project manager and salesman. In 1989, we broke ground and selected Thomas McBroom as our architect.

"Tom and I worked well together. We both felt that the land itself should dictate the routing of the course. The course far exceeded our expectations."

The first hole is a short par 5 characterized by a waste bunker that runs down the right side of the fairway. The second or third shot must carry a large gorge and creek to an elevated, well-bunkered green. A canyon-like effect is created by mounds surrounding the perimeter of the hole. Number 2 is one of the most demanding holes at Camelot: the tee shot must carry a creek on the left side of the fairway while the second shot must avoid a large pond on the left. The third requires a tee shot between two large lakes and the par-3 fourth challenges the player to carry part of a lake in front of the large, well-protected green.

Number 5 can only be described as a spectacular par 5. From an elevated tee, the player must choose between two fairways: the shorter route crosses a series of bunkers guarding the left side and the second shot must avoid fairway bunkers lining the ever-narrowing fairway. The tree-line sixth hole

The fourth green is tucked dangerously behind a pond.

plays uphill to a large, open green. An apple orchard is home to the beautiful par-3 seventh hole. The green is perched on the edge of a very steep ravine, so it won't do to be long or left here.

The eighth hole is described as short but treacherous. The tee shot must reach the corner of the dogleg and the second shot must carry a gorge. Number 9 is visually stunning: the tee shot is played from an elevated tee which affords a panoramic view of the countryside. The second shot from the valley floor must carry all the way to the large elevated double green which serves both the ninth and 18th holes.

The back nine commences with a medium-length par 5 which plays into the prevailing wind. The long par-3 11th hole plays downhill across a gorge and Number 12 is the toughest on the course (see sidebar). It is followed by the most challenging par 4 at Camelot. This dogleg left boasts an approach shot played through a chute of trees to an elevated green. Fourteen may be the most interesting par 4 on the course, offering an option: the dogleg left can be cut if the player has the courage and the length to avoid the bunkers on the corner, or you can play to the wide part of the fairway, leaving a mid-iron to the elevated, well-bunkered green.

After the 187-yard par-3 15th hole, you are presented with Number 16 — a great short par 5 presenting three targets that must be hit. The tee shot must be played down the right side and the second shot must be played to the left side to allow for the best view of the green which is on a ledge, surrounded by trouble. The 17th is the shortest hole at Camelot, but compensates for that with a very undulating green. And your round concludes with a classic finishing hole. The 18th is a magnificent par 4, playing from an elevated tee into a beautiful valley and then back up to the spectacular double green.

The Toughest Hole at Camelot

"You have to hit a cannon off this tee in order to be in position to hit the second landing area," says course architect Tom McBroom of the par-5 12th hole at Camelot. "The second shot will be a three-wood or long iron over a rise that is guarded by bunkers. The third shot is a wedge into a tiny green that is bunkered on each side. Length and accuracy are a must. It's not a hole you try to birdie."

The par-3 11th is long but plays downhill across a gorge.

The 16th tee at Credit Valley, a classic members' course.

CREDIT VALLEY

Golf Club

Architects: *Stanley Thompson, C.E. (Robbie) Robinson, Doug Carrick*
Head Professional: *Charles Slaughter*
General Manager: *Darryl Abbott*
Superintendent: *Doug Suter*

When providing background material to be used in this book, Credit Valley member Bill Newton wrote the following to the author:

"We want to leave the impression that Credit Valley is a friendly, people-driven environment; has a solid reputation and a most interesting history with an emphasis on tradition; is accessible in both location and in the sense that it does not present itself as aloof or elitist. It is family oriented, a modern self-contained facility; a property which is not only maintained to the highest standards, but is a natural environment; and a course which is a fine test of golf in the championship mode."

One could not imagine a more concise or comprehensive outline for a story on Credit Valley Golf Club, whose motto is "A golfing tradition since the 1930s." While golf has indeed been played on this site for some 60 years, it has been played in several variations.

The original clubhouse overlooking the scenic Credit River valley was the summer home of Ontario Lieutenant Governor William Donald Ross. Ross followed the construction of his retreat

in 1930 with the building of a six-hole private course. Not one to do things by halves, Ross procured the services of the renowned architect Stanley Thompson, whose talents are evident in courses ranging from Banff Springs in the Rockies to Highland Links on Cape Breton Island. After Ross's term ended in 1932, it was transformed into a nine-hole pay-as-you-play facility, again with design assistance from Thompson. In 1943, it was sold and evolved into a public course with memberships.

In 1951, the members leased the property and decided to apply for a charter to operate as a membership club. Shortly thereafter, the course was expanded to an unconventional 13 holes, a situation which lasted until five more holes were added in 1954 to round out the count to 18. That same year, the course was devastated by Hurricane Hazel but, undeterred, the members repaired the course and built a new clubhouse, which now serves as a turf and administration centre.

In the late 1950s, Credit Valley rounded into its final stage when the course became fully member-owned and private and the property was purchased. In 1969, the club purchased substantial land in the river valley. After selling some of its tableland property, the design and construction of the present layout and clubhouse was undertaken. Robbie Robinson, one of Thompson's disciples, became the architect of record at this time. As he surveyed the property, he observed that he "had never seen a more perfect

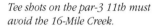

Tee shots on the par-3 11th must avoid the 16-Mile Creek.

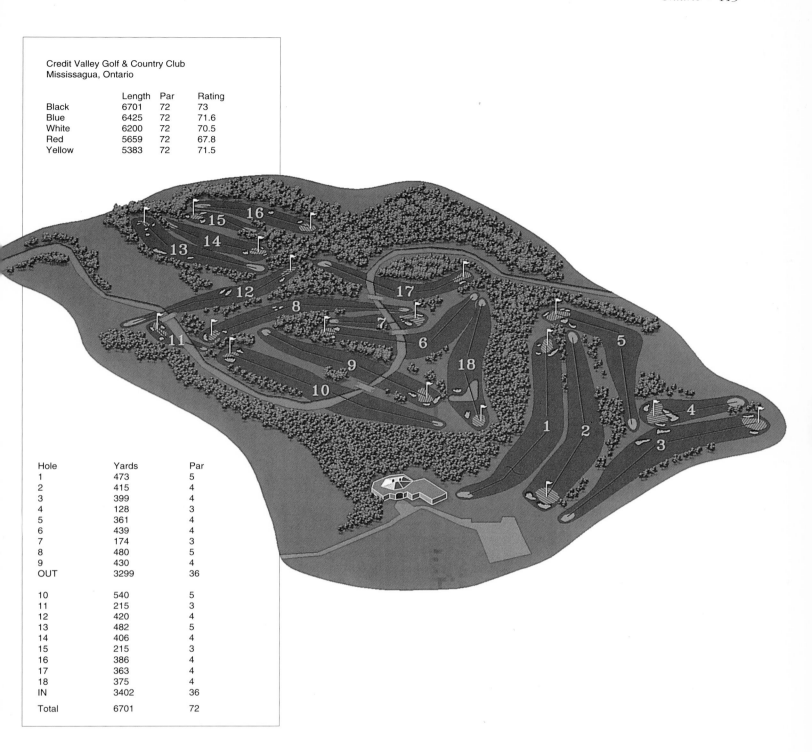

Credit Valley Golf & Country Club
Mississagua, Ontario

	Length	Par	Rating
Black	6701	72	73
Blue	6425	72	71.6
White	6200	72	70.5
Red	5659	72	67.8
Yellow	5383	72	71.5

Hole	Yards	Par
1	473	5
2	415	4
3	399	4
4	128	3
5	361	4
6	439	4
7	174	3
8	480	5
9	430	4
OUT	3299	36
10	540	5
11	215	3
12	420	4
13	482	5
14	406	4
15	215	3
16	386	4
17	363	4
18	375	4
IN	3402	36
Total	6701	72

natural setting for a golf course." In turn, Robinson's protege, Doug Carrick of Toronto, is preparing a master plan for the property. As in all things at Credit Valley, continuity and an innate respect for tradition are essential.

Again, Bill Newton uses his powers of summation: "Credit Valley has undergone many crises including Hurricane Hazel and a major flood in the '70s. It is a major rags to riches story where members, through perseverance and dedication, established this golf course as one of the finest in the country. Today, the club is not only well established and highly regarded as a golf course, it is debt free. Members remain hardworking, loyal and appreciative of the club's history and attributes."

Credit Valley is one of a few clubs which remain attuned to the needs of all family groups: juniors, intermediates, seniors, spouses, men and women. Spousal play is encouraged as is a junior program, conspicuous by its vigor. Most members are competitive golfers and Credit Valley has more than its share of low-handicappers. The first tee is generally busy although good management prevents overcrowding or back-ups. Mem-

"A GOLFING TRADITION SINCE THE 1930s"

Credit Valley member Bill Newton has lent his creative powers to names for every hole, some of which reveal the course's rich history and others of which are simply amusing:

Hole #1 *Guvernor's Estate*

The family of Lieutenant Governor W.D. Ross owned the club's original property. In the early 1930s, he built a six-hole course at this summer retreat for play by family and friends.

Hole #5 *Tribute to Al*

Al Balding, now a member of the Canadian Golf Hall of Fame, was the club's first professional in 1954. During his tenure, owner Art Price encouraged him to go on the PGA Tour. Balding heeded the advice and went on to become one of Canada's best and most respected golfers.

Hole #15 *Matrimonial Bliss*

The competitive play of couples has always been encouraged. Since the 1950s, the Matrimonial Tournament has been popular. No divorces have been reported as a result, but some couples have been known to leave the property immediately after their round.

Hole #18 (shown below) *Priceless Legacy*

Arthur Price is the father of Credit Valley. He leased the Ross property in the early 1930s for the purpose of public play. In 1943, he purchased it and continued to operate a nine-hole pay-as-you-play with memberships at a nominal fee. Then, in 1951, he leased the property to about 100 members who applied for a private membership charter. Although the course still operated with public play and was extended to 13 holes, the die was cast. In the late '50s, the club became private. Art's vision has become his legacy.

bership is varied, covering the spectrum of age groups, occupations and backgrounds, and a visitor or new member is all but assured of a warm greeting in the clubhouse or on the tee.

The clubhouse is clad in wood, a modern design which nestles into a hill, and features a spectacular view overlooking the river valley. Aside from boasting one of the best pro shops in the region, the facility offers an indoor pool and fully equipped health club.

Despite its location within minutes of the core of Toronto, golfers are still treated to the sight of deer and many species of birds. Salmon battle their way upstream, and the valley setting provides eyecatching vistas of steep river embankments.

Thirteen of the holes stretch along the river valley, with the remaining five resting on the tablelands. The greens are extremely fast and tricky, with the river coming into play on eight holes.

The dogleg-right par-4 6th hole is rated the tougest on the course.

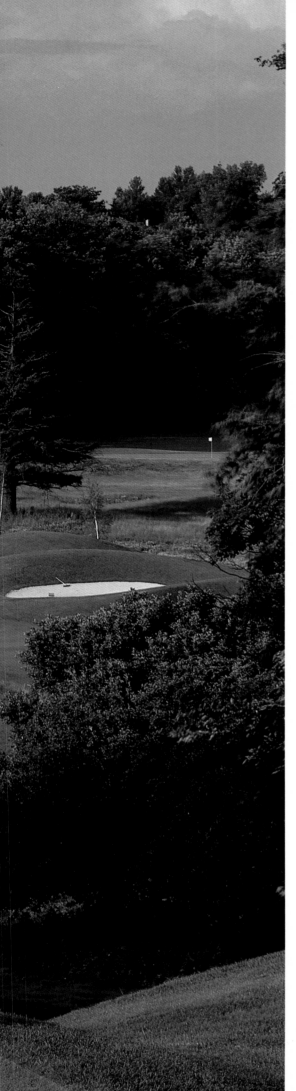

The 16th is a par 3 of 202 yards from a tee perched atop a valley wall to a green sitting on the edge of a large lake below.

DEER RIDGE

Golf Club

Architect: Thomas McBroom
Golf Director: Gus Maue
Associate Professional: Ron Silver
Administrator: Kerry Barnum
Superintendent: Greg Aljoe

Skirting the meandering Grand River near Kitchener, Ontario is one of Canada's finest new courses — Deer Ridge Golf Club. Masterfully designed by Thomas McBroom of Toronto, now established as one of the top course architects in North America, Deer Ridge offers a challenging and rewarding experience to golfers of all handicaps.

Deer Ridge could be called "state of the art" for several reasons. The first is the expansive, multi-featured practice area offering target greens and practice bunkers. Another would be the way McBroom has structured the well-balanced layout to take full advantage of the floodplain and bluffs nestled against the Grand River. The course was developed with the guidance of the Grand River Conservation Authority to preserve the environmental integrity of the area. The success of this approach is evident to players who are startled by the sight of curious deer poking their heads out of the forest or the splashing of fish in several small ponds.

McBroom says not only was he given 200 acres of great property to work with, but "the owners at Deer Ridge gave me a budget that

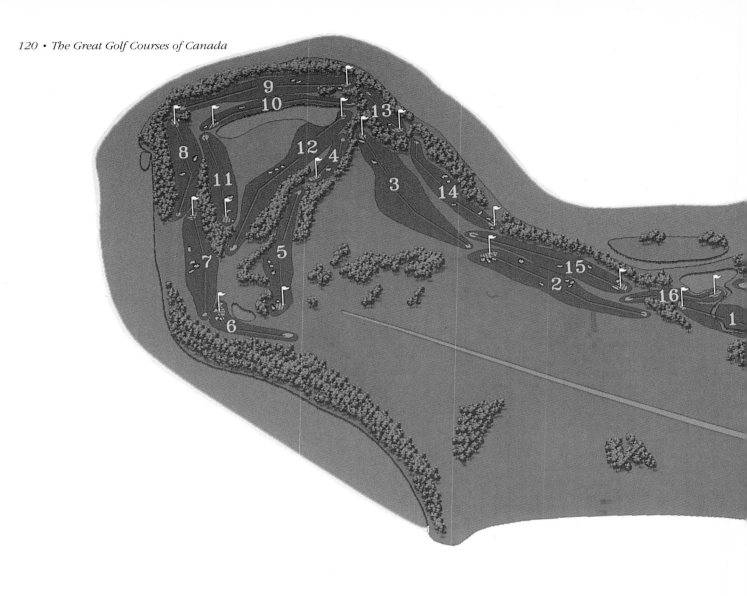

allowed me to design a course comparable to the best courses in North America, and we have accomplished this."

While the pros and adventurous amateurs might trudge back to the tips and play Deer Ridge at its full 7,200 yards (a pro tournament held in the course's infancy drew rave reviews from the participants, including the legendary Al Balding), most golfers would benefit from playing it somewhere between that Herculean length and a more sensible 6,100 yards.

"Deer Ridge is a bit unique in that it offers a non-returning route — nine holes out and nine holes back in," says McBroom. "The fact that it was built entirely on the Grand River floodplain created quite an engineering challenge and you could say what we did at Deer Ridge rewrote the book on this kind of development.

"We raised all the tees, greens and fairways from three to six feet using only on-site fill. All the playable areas are perched, or raised, using the fill we took from the ponds on site. This gives the golf course

excellent drainage." While the course is PGA Tour length from the back tees, McBroom says it plays shorter than the numbers would indicate: "It's flattish and you get tremendous roll; it's something like a desert course."

Only 400 full-equity memberships will be sold in this zero-debt club, and those members will be rewarded by being able to tee off without pre-booking times (except on weekend mornings). According to Golf Director Gus Maue, members should complete their rounds in 3 1/2 hours or less.

Maue, a golf professional since 1961, spent 23 years at Kitchener's venerable Westmount Golf and Country Club, one of the country's best. After retiring from Westmount, he says it took a very special opportunity to persuade him to get back into the business. "I feel very fortunate to have been given the opportunity to work with a small group of local investors in pioneering and building a new golf club that will have the potential of ranking with the best courses in Canada."

Maue was joined in the early going by

Deer Ridge Golf Club
Kitchener, Ontario

	Length	Par	Rating
Gold	7093	72	74.9
Blue	6552	72	72.2
White	6055	72	69.8
Red	5344	72	67

Hole	Yards	Par			
1	531	5	10	392	4
2	456	4	11	346	4
3	591	5	12	568	5
4	168	3	13	162	3
5	438	4	14	433	4
6	220	3	15	389	4
7	389	4	16	213	3
8	403	4	17	446	4
9	453	4	18	495	5
OUT	3649	36	IN	3444	36
			Total	7093	72

The 10th is a mid-length par 4 of 390 yards with a large lake stretching up the left side from tee to green.

The 6th hole is the most difficult of the par 3s at Deer Ridge, a 206-yarder across a small lake to a narrow green.

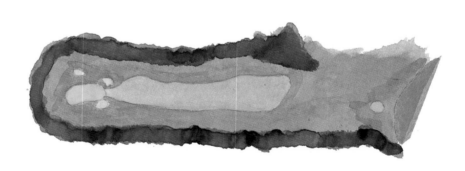

Toughest Hole at Deer Ridge

The 17th at Deer Ridge rates as the hardest hole on the course, according to Thomas McBroom, the architect responsible for this admirable layout and a low-handicap golfer himself. "Seventeen is a very tough driving hole. You must be long to have a chance at hitting the green in two. The crowned fairway falls away on the sides, so you have to be right down the middle. Then you're hitting a long iron to a long, narrow, raised green. Club selection is vital – if you guess wrong, you could have a 100-foot putt. The green is surrounded by bunkers and grassy hollows, but the putting surface is not greatly contoured."

amateur legend turned pro, Gary Cowan, a Kitchener native. Cowan assisted in the marketing of Deer Ridge and represented the club while competing in tournaments on the Senior PGA Tour circuit in the United States.

Like several other fine courses in southern Ontario, Deer Ridge has taken the equity membership route. Under this plan, each member owns an equal share of the golf course, the land it is built on and all its physical assets. Deer Ridge, the first significant addition to the Kitchener golf scene in decades, had success with the marketing plan which appeals to individual and corporate members. If the member leaves the club for any reason, the membership may be sold, leased or otherwise transferred. If the club is sold, the members share equally in the proceeds.

The Deer Ridge clubhouse blends into the scenery as naturally as the course melds with the landscape. Handsomely appointed in oak, maple, granite and marble, it is a true "members" clubhouse rich in understated elegance. The luxurious games room and spacious lounge promise to become a second home to many members.

All in all, the developers of Deer Ridge appear to have accomplished the lofty goals they set when writing the club's concept statement: "Deer Ridge Golf Club is intended to be an exclusive, businesspersons' golf course, owned by its members, for its members. Deer Ridge is dedicated to serious golfers who value liberal accessibility to the first tee for themselves and their guests in order to enjoy a well-manicured, secluded golf course offering a fair test of golfing skill. Deer Ridge is intended to be operated by professional management, and not by a committee, with a minimum amount of regulation and a maximum amount of flexibility, within the bounds of reason."

At 500 yards, the 18th is an extraordinary finishing hole, offering birdie potential for two precisely struck shots.

The par-5 14th at Deerhurst Highlands is reachable in two.

DEERHURST HIGHLANDS

Golf Club

Architects:Robert Cupp, Thomas McBroom
Head Professional: Paul Kennedy
Superintendent: Ed Farnsworth

Deerhurst Highlands defines golf in Canada. Winding its majestic way through the ancient forest crowning the craggy Canadian Shield, skirting lakes and streams, this 7,000-yard jewel holds its own with any course in Canada.

Part of the posh four-season Deerhurst Resort (which also boasts an 18-hole, 4,700-yard, par-65 layout in addition to almost every other recreational activity) in the rugged Muskoka region 250 kilometres north of Toronto, the Highlands speaks volumes about the design talents of American Bob Cupp and Toronto's Tom McBroom.

While the strength of the property was based on the unique topography of the Shield, the location also posed many problems, McBroom says. "Deerhurst is built on solid rock. It's comparable in many ways to Banff Springs, which was built in the Rocky Mountains in the 1920s, and was the first course to cost more than $1 million to build. Every cubic inch of topsoil and subsoil had to be brought in." Costruction required the importation of about 15,000 truckloads of sand alone.

Head pro Paul Kennedy calls Deerhurst, which had its first

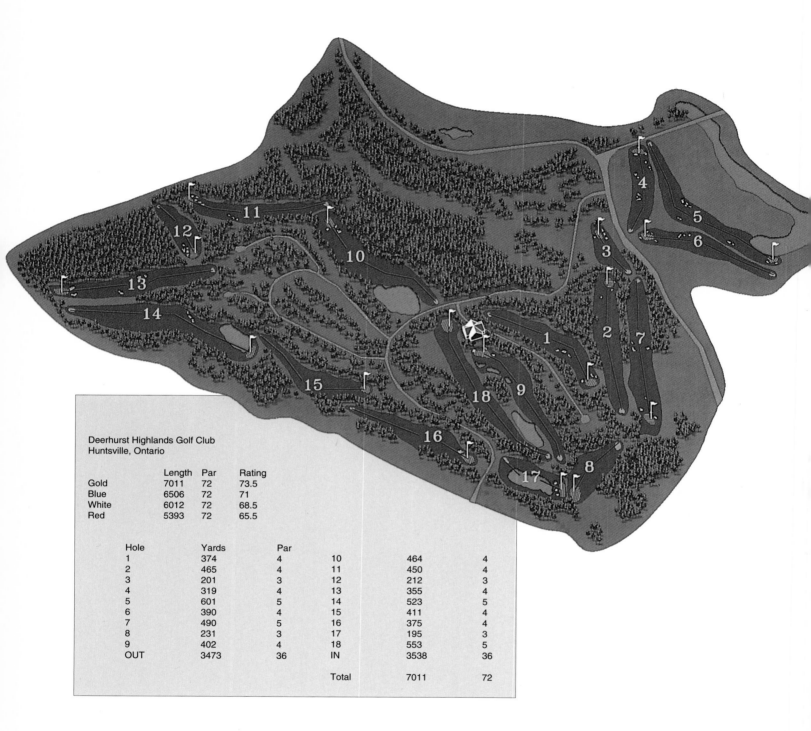

Deerhurst Highlands Golf Club
Huntsville, Ontario

	Length	Par	Rating
Gold	7011	72	73.5
Blue	6506	72	71
White	6012	72	68.5
Red	5393	72	65.5

Hole	Yards	Par			
1	374	4	10	464	4
2	465	4	11	450	4
3	201	3	12	212	3
4	319	4	13	355	4
5	601	5	14	523	5
6	390	4	15	411	4
7	490	5	16	375	4
8	231	3	17	195	3
9	402	4	18	553	5
OUT	3473	36	IN	3538	36
			Total	7011	72

full season in 1991, "a course to challenge the pros and yet, with four different tee blocks, everyone can enjoy it." Kennedy knows whereof he speaks: one of the top pros on the Canadian Tour for years, he won the Canadian Club Pro Championship in 1984 and has been assisting golfers at Deerhurst since 1982.

McBroom also advises visitors (while there is a membership structure, the course is open to the public, although resort guests get a discounted fee) to play the correct tees in order to maximize their enjoyment. "The course is only 6,000 yards from the whites and it's not as intimidating as it looks. We've cleared the fairways extra-wide for the benefit of the occasional golfer and the greens are not severe."

"This is the quintessential Canadian golf course," says the justifiably proud McBroom who previously teamed with Cupp, the design consultant at Augusta National, on the acclaimed Beacon Hall in Aurora, Ontario. Both have impressive individual portfolios as well. "I'm very proud of the way the routing takes advantage of the land. The fit with the natural landscape is strong."

As proof, he cites the second hole, where a straight tee shot is required to clear a sheer 60-foot-high rock face and attain the landing area. But, assures McBroom, "it's not as intimidating as it looks. It's a 185-yard carry from the golds and about 170 from the blues. The trick is to put the visuals out of your mind and swing easy." Despite those reassuring words, the architect calls this hole the most difficult on the course. The second shot is slightly uphill to a green that is not visible, yet the position of the flagstick is obvious. The green, says McBroom, "is large and has three levels. Its saving grace is that it is not bunkered." There are several grassy hollows protecting the putting surface.

The architects say this hole forewarns the player of a concept consistent throughout their design. "At Deerhurst, the rock becomes a major element in the theme of the golf course design. Although never in play, it poses a menacing threat." As McBroom says, disregard the implied threat and swing easy.

The theme reappears on other holes — reinforced with the notations "cliff", "rock" or "boulders" in the course guide — but most notably holes 3, 10 (see sidebar), 12 and 18.

The 12th, a long par 3, features a vertical granite face providing the left backdrop for the green. "The trick is to carry a strategically placed bunker set some 10 yards in front of the green," say the architects. "This bunker will create the illusion of making the putting surface appear closer than it really is. Club selection is paramount."

On 18, use the massive boulder on the left side of the fairway as your target. "Consistent with the concluding holes at many of the world's great golf courses," the architects say, "the 18th hole at Deerhurst demands a long and well-placed tee shot, preferably drawn

Water, rock and forest — all part of the character of Deerhurst Highlands.

Fade your tee shot on Number 11 for the best approach to its angled green.

into a very slight upslope. Designed so as not to be reachable in two, it may still be possible with the execution of an extraordinary tee shot. The second shot is through a long chute bordered by the ninth fairway to the right and a grassy upslope on the left. Cutting in front of the green is a boulder-strewn creek with a series of pools and waterfalls. The perfect second shot must either carry the creek to the putting surface beyond or be positioned short of it. The putting surface is a mass of beautiful swirling contours and will surrender to only the most skilled of shotmakers."

The course complements one of the finest four-season resorts anywhere. Built in 1896 as a fishing lodge by Englishman Charles Waterhouse, Deerhurst now boasts a 110,000 square-foot state-of-the-art complex housing racquet sports, spa, pro shops, pool, conference room and other amenities. Accommodations are varied and first-class.

Deerhurst Highlands rounds out an impressive roster of properties under the umbrella of Canadian Pacific Hotels and Resorts, the largest single owner and operator of golf courses in Canada. Others include Alberta's Banff Springs and Jasper Park Lodge, Chateau Montebello in Quebec, the Algonquin (St. Andrews By-The-Sea, N.B.) and Chateau Whistler (and its brand-new Robert Trent Jones Jr. course), a couple of hours north of Vancouver.

The Signature Hole at Deerhurst Highlands

A descriptive narrative, written by architects Bob Cupp and Tom McBroom, describes the 10th hole: "Designed by Mother Nature, with a small assist from the architects, this hole is arguably one of the prettiest and most demanding in the world. From tees high atop a rocky ridge, the drive must carry a large lake to a perched landing area. Dominating the view from the tee is a vertical granite wall with fairway below and to the left and virgin woods to the right. The tee shot must be long and straight. Visibility of the putting surface is guaranteed only with a drive of 260 yards from the gold tees. The approach to a complex multitiered green is through a nest of cross bunkers."

Pick the right club and aim for the centre of the green on the par-3 8th hole.

The back nine at Devil's Pulpit begins with this spectacular par 4.

DEVIL'S PULPIT

Golf Association

Architect: Michael Hurdzan
Director of Golf: Doug Ball
Head Professional: Ken Trowbridge
General Manager: Dave McDonald
Superintendent: Ken Wright

On January 7, 1989, a couple of hundred golf nuts gathered in a community centre northwest of Toronto to spend thousands of dollars to join a golf course that existed only on paper. Why the excitement? Because the course was the brainchild of Chris Haney and Scott Abbott — inventors of the wildly successful board game Trivial Pursuit.

The fact that the Devil's Pulpit (named after a rock formation visible from the course) was many months away from completion deterred neither the prospective members nor Doug Ball, the Pulpit's director of golf. All were banking that Haney and Abbott retained the Midas touch that made them and their Trivial Pursuit investors millionaires.

Surprisingly, Ball, an award-winning news photographer who met Haney and Abbott during their previous lives as journalists, did not buy a share of the board game when it was offered. But he jumped at the chance to work at Devil's Pulpit: "I've never been this excited about anything in my life — except the birth of my sons," he said at the time. "I missed getting in on Trivial Pursuit, but the bus stopped twice in my case."

Like the Trivial Pursuit investors, those early believers have been proven right many times over — the course, designed by Michael Hurdzan, and the clubhouse are world-class and have received unparalleled acclaim. The crowning touch came when the highly respected U.S. publication Golf Digest anointed the Pulpit "the best new private course in Canada" in 1992.

(In an unprecedented "one-two" punch, the Pulpit's sister course, the Devil's Paintbrush, was selected by Golf Digest as "best new private course in Canada" in 1993. The Paintbrush, located five kilometres away, was designed by Hurdzan in a links style. "Just like Scotland without the North Sea,"

says Haney.)

The two courses combine to create for their extremely fortunate members a golf facility which is unique in the world. The Pulpit, built on 315 acres in the Caledon Hills some 70 kilometres northwest of Toronto, offers a multi-faceted, larger-than-life golf experience which delights the average player and challenges the scratch amateur or pro.

Transferable memberships offer privileges at both courses and the number will be capped at 750. For those who may not have the thrill of a lifetime, here's a brief hole-by-hole narrative from Doug Ball:

The first hole offers a warm-up opportunity since many players probably can't

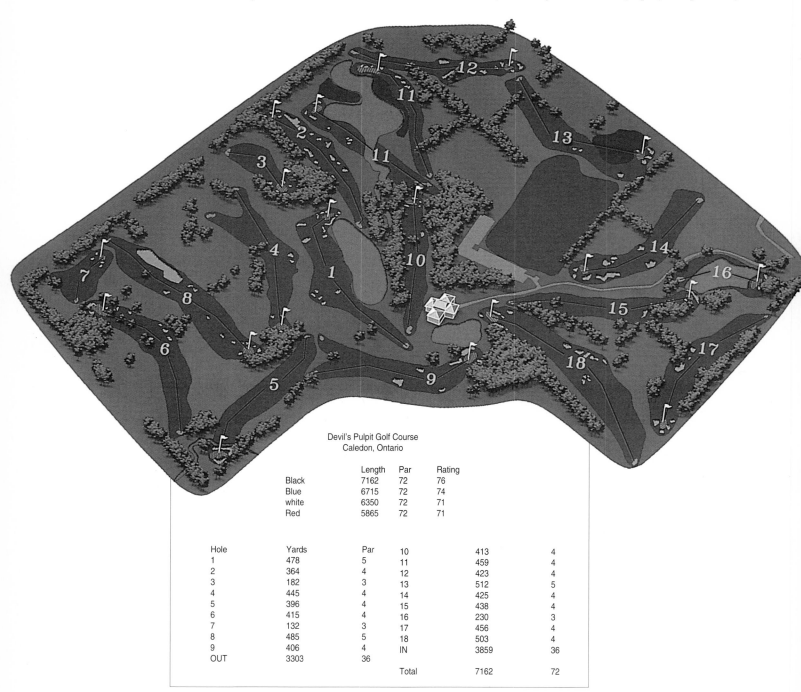

Devil's Pulpit Golf Course
Caledon, Ontario

	Length	Par	Rating
Black	7162	72	76
Blue	6715	72	74
white	6350	72	71
Red	5865	72	71

Hole	Yards	Par			
1	478	5	10	413	4
2	364	4	11	459	4
3	182	3	12	423	4
4	445	4	13	512	5
5	396	4	14	425	4
6	415	4	15	438	4
7	132	3	16	230	3
8	485	5	17	456	4
9	406	4	18	503	4
OUT	3303	36	IN	3859	36
			Total	7162	72

concentrate because they are bowled over by the scenery (see sidebar). The second is a short par-4. Hit an iron off the tee to afford you a full shot into a green that slopes away. The three-lobed green of the par-3 third is nestled in a treed amphitheatre and requires anything from an eight-iron to a four-iron.

Number 4 is a long, uphill dogleg right that plays into the prevailing wind. Note the unique timber-backed bunker behind the large green. The fifth hole calls for a blind tee shot about 230 yards down the right side, leaving a full shot to a shallow green wedged between a creek and bunkers in front and wasteland behind. If you hit your drive into the graveyard on the left side of the sixth hole, you are entitled to a free

drop. The Pulpit's namesake hole, Number 7, shows that length is often overrated as a measure of a hole's true merit. This 132-yard par-3 demands a near-perfect shot to surrender a par, much less a birdie.

A great drive on Number 8 will set you up to get home in two, but remember the green slopes severely from back to front. On Number 9, the pin position dictates the length of the ideal drive. If the pin is front right, lay off the driver a touch; if the flag is back left, let it fly. This green is four clubs deep.

The 10th hole possesses the world's biggest 150-yard marker: a towering tree exactly 150 paces from the middle of the green. An elevated tee provides a great view of this narrow fairway tracing its way through a tree-lined valley. On Number 11, you must

The dogleg-left ninth hole has a green that is four clubs deep.

There are actually two 11th holes a the Pulpit, encircling a small lake.

carry 252 yards to get to the fairway from the championship tees. Stay left of the 150-yard marker to get the best angle into the green. Avoid the bunker in the middle of the double green which also serves the par-3 betting hole. And while you're there, check out the "other" 11th hole on the other side of the lake — that's right, this golf course has 20 holes.

Number 12 plays uphill into the wind and calls for the driver. On 13, a good drive will set up a long iron or fairway wood over a pond and waste bunker into a shallow green. The ideal tee shot on 14 is a driver right of the sod-wall bunkers and then a mid-iron in. The 15th is a difficult driving hole and only a well-struck ball will make it over the waste area to the fairway.

Sixteen is a monster par 3 over a lake. Although there is a bailout area on the right, a far-left pin position means the tee shot is all carry. The 17th calls for a driver to the right-centre of the fairway followed by a mid-iron to a large green. Number 18 is a great par-4 finishing hole; a long drive and an accurate long iron can cap your day off with a birdie.

Although a very young course, Devil's Pulpit has tested — and bested in most cases — some excellent players from around the world in the Canadian Tour's Tournament Players Championship. It has also played host to the RCGA's Canadian Club Champions Championship and was scheduled to be a Canadian Open qualifying site in 1993.

The Legendary First Hole at Devil's Pulpit

There are many golf courses in the world which have not had as much said or written about them as the first hole at Devil's Pulpit. When BMW selected an "ultimate" golf hole for its advertising campaign, it chose the opening hole at the Pulpit. As course architect Michael Hurdzan explains: "Perhaps no other golf hole in the world more clearly proves that first impressions are lasting impressions. The first tee at Devil's Pulpit overlooks an awesome collage of dramatic golf features in the foreground, farmland in the middle ground, and a backdrop of Toronto's skyline 35 miles away. The hole is named the Tower Hole because the aiming point for most tee shots is the CN Tower. The tee shot drops 60 feet to the wide, contoured members' fairway, or to an alternate narrow fairway sandwiched between a huge hemlock on the left and a lake on the right. From the members' fairway, Number 1 is a comfortable par 5, while from the 'pro' fairway an accurate four- or five-iron leaves a putt for eagle. My clients, Chris Haney and Scott Abbott, creators of Trivial Pursuit, wanted a dramatic golf course with panoramic vistas. The first hole was evident the minute I saw it, but creating it was extremely difficult. Fifteen acres of additional land had to be purchased. Then we had to move 300,000 cubic yards of earth (enough to build a modest 18-hole course) and build a pond on a hillside. The cost was estimated at $1.6 million. Players are presented with limitless options to master the hole — the purest form of strategic design — with the beauty of the flawless grooming that modern technology allows."

*Like many holes at Emerald Hills, both sides of
the 12th fairway are lined with hazards.*

EMERALD HILLS

Golf and Country Club

Architect: Rene Muylaert
Head Professional: Greg Seemann
General Manager: Bill Johnson
Superintendent: Brian Halls

"Sculpted from the natural divide between Lake Ontario and Lake
Simcoe, Emerald Hills is a blend of rolling fairways, hardwood
forest and spring-fed ponds," say enthusiasts of this hidden gem
north of Toronto. Founded in 1982 by longtime CPGA pro Harry
Allard, who was deeply involved in its design and construction,
Emerald Hills is a relatively unheralded course which follows
the glacier-formed contours of the Oak Ridges moraine.

Emerald Hills is a players' course, having provided a challenge
to numerous tournaments, including the 1988 Canadian Professional Golfers' Association Championship, won by Brent Franklin.
The one-round tournament record is 67, by Dave Barr of
Richmond, B.C. Maintained to exacting standards and always
ready to play host to championship events, this golf course dictates
intelligent shot-making if you want to score well.

Holes one to nine, longer and more open, are a driver's course;
whereas the back nine is narrower and demands accuracy. Head pro
Greg Seemann says "the strengths of the course are the par 3s, the
first four holes, Number 6 and the final three holes."

The first four holes, one of Seemann's measures of the course,

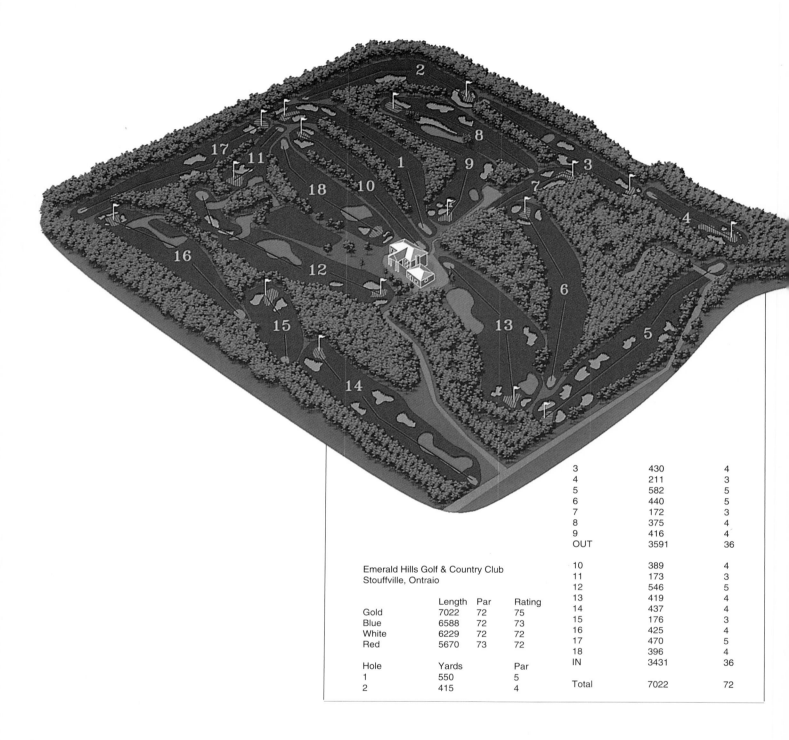

Emerald Hills Golf & Country Club
Stouffville, Ontraio

	Length	Par	Rating
Gold	7022	72	75
Blue	6588	72	73
White	6229	72	72
Red	5670	73	72

Hole	Yards	Par
1	550	5
2	415	4
3	430	4
4	211	3
5	582	5
6	440	5
7	172	3
8	375	4
9	416	4
OUT	3591	36
10	389	4
11	173	3
12	546	5
13	419	4
14	437	4
15	176	3
16	425	4
17	470	5
18	396	4
IN	3431	36
Total	7022	72

start with a true three-shot par 5, a gently sweeping dogleg left. The tee shot is made to a progressively narrowing landing area. A long drive which threads the needle may set up an easy birdie, while a short or erratic tee shot all but guarantees a big number. A conservative second shot to the left side of the fairway will leave a wedge into the well-bunkered green which is also guarded by mature maples on the left side.

The second hole is a severe dogleg right, with a cavernous bunker tucked in the corner of the dogleg. The ideal tee shot will hug the right side of the fairway, getting as close as possible to the bunkers. Accuracy is the key to allow a mid to short iron into the green wedged between bunkers front, back and left.

Number 3 is a straightaway par 4 with a huge fairway bunker lurking on the left side. Length is vital to score well on this hole which usually plays into the prevailing west winds. A long drive sets up a mid iron into a wide but shallow green.

The fourth hole is the first opportunity

to play one of Emerald Hills' par 3s, of which Seemann is justifiably proud. At 181 yards from the blue tees, the fourth requires both accuracy and length. The green gradually works back from left to right and is adjacent to a large bunker dotted with several islands.

This hole description also provides an opportunity to segue into an outline of the other par 3s: numbers 7, 11 and 15. The seventh is not long at 142 yards from the blue tees, but presents a challenge nonetheless. The large green provides for a multitude of pin positions, making club selection a test. The deep bunker fronting the green presents another mental hurdle as well. The 11th, at 154 from the blues, is characterized by the large pond that starts in the left side of the green and wraps itself around the front third of the putting

Hitting an iron off the tee may be the answer to the par-5 12th hole.

surface. Thick forest stands ready on the right side of the hole to swallow errant tee shots. Seemann advises you to disregard the visual distractions, stay calm and aim for the centre of the green. Be satisfied with pars on the one-shotters at Emerald Hills.

The homestretch here commences with Number 15, a deceptively simple par 3 which offers a fine view from an elevated tee to a roller-coaster green flanked by large multi-lobed bunkers.

"The real test of the back nine starts on 16," says Seemann. "The key here is keeping the ball in play." The 16th requires a "thread-the-needle" tee shot, perhaps with a long iron, to avoid the hazards on either side of the fairway. The subtly mounded green, in the shape of a figure-8, awaits on the other side of yet another pond. Caution, and prudent club selection, are advisable here.

Seventeen has brought many a player to grief and par is usually elusive. The narrow fairway snakes between forest on the right and out of bounds and bunkers left. While not long, it requires precision to hit and stay on the smallish, elevated green. "This is a real teaser," the pro says. "Played as a three-shot par 5, par can be an easy score. The aggressive golfer can be rewarded with an easy birdie, or even an eagle, but also be prepared for a double bogey or worse."

The 18th, a dogleg left, requires a long iron or fairway wood off the tee. The second shot must carry a black reflecting pool which is about 30 yards short of the well-bunkered elevated green presided over by the elegant clubhouse.

Number 16 marks the start of the great finishing holes at Emerald Hills.

Ignore the trouble on Number 11 and aim for the middle of the green.

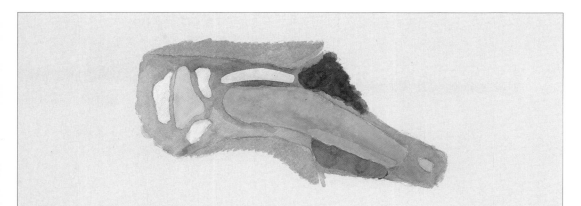

The Toughest Hole at Emerald Hills

After negotiating the four tough opening holes at Emerald Hills, the player is granted a respite on the fifth before facing what head professional Greg Seemann rates as the most difficult test on the course. The sixth, 440 yards from the gold tees, is rated the Number 1 stroke hole. It is a long dogleg par 4 defined by lateral water hazards on both sides and deep greenside bunkers. "This hole requires it all," says Seemann, "length and accuracy off the tee, and then an accurate mid to long iron into a guarded green. Tucked pin placements can make this hole a true monster."

Perhaps Glen Abbey's most spectacular sight: from the 11th tee, players hit into a river valley some 120 feet below.

GLEN ABBEY

Golf Club

Architect: Jack Nicklaus
Head Professional: Bob Lean
Manager: Jack McClellan
Superintendent: Dean Baker

"The shrine of Canadian golf." Perhaps that is putting it a bit strongly, but there is no doubt that Glen Abbey Golf Club is more, much more, than just another public golf course.

The "shrine" phrase first appears in press reports about plans put forth in the early 1970s by the Royal Canadian Golf Association and Great Northern Capital Inc. to develop a permanent site for the Canadian Open, the world's fourth-oldest national championship, hosted by the RCGA. The association's headquarters would be on the site, housing the offices of the people who govern organized amateur golf in this country as well as the Canadian Golf Hall of Fame and Museum.

The religious analogy might have been encouraged not only by the fact that the existing building on the site north of Oakville, Ontario, had been used as a Jesuit retreat, but also by the "golfing god" contracted to design the course: the legendary Jack Nicklaus.

Richard Grimm, now the RCGA's director of professional tournaments, was the organization's president back in 1972 and had acted as chairman of the Open which was held that year at Cherry Hill near Fort Erie, Ontario. When approached by Rod McIsaac of Great Northern, Grimm was leery. "He told me he liked watching the tournament, but it was his feeling that the gallery was not given a fair shake for viewing," Grimm recalled later. "Immediately I thought, 'Here's another gripe from a spectator.' But then he threw me a country mile by saying he had a piece of property in Oakville — and we were thinking about a permanent site. The result of that conversation was meetings with the RCGA, Jack Nicklaus, the Abbey Glen Property Corporation and Imperial Tobacco Limited (longtime sponsors of the Open), and the result of those meetings was Glen Abbey." That "result" has played host to every Canadian Open since 1977, with the exception of 1980 when the national championship was played at Royal Montreal.

When McIsaac made his proposal, more than 200 acres remained of the 350 that mining magnate Andre Dorfman purchased in 1929 to build an imposing castle-like home for himself and his new wife. Sold in 1953 to the Jesuits, it became available later when Rome ruled that the priests could better serve the church in Toronto. Some of the land was already used for golf, but the layout was unsuitable for the national championship.

Nicklaus, whose professional career was at its peak, had decided to lend his talent to golf course architecture. What he was faced with at Glen Abbey, the first design project he had undertaken on his own, was a schizophrenic situation: most of the land was flat and relatively undistinguished, but the remainder was wonderful river valley land snaking along the meandering Sixteen Mile Creek in the shadow of spectacular bluffs.

More than one million cubic feet of earth were moved to massage the flat land into a fine test of golf, "a panorama of gently rolling fairways," in Nicklaus's words. In excess of 100,000 cubic yards of topsoil became mounds, designed to give spectators at Glen Abbey the

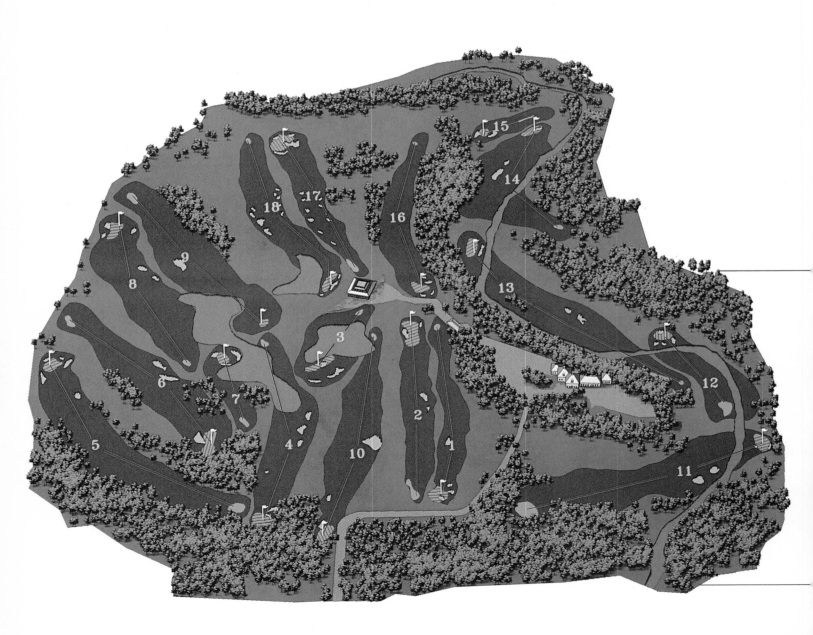

The par-four 14th is considered one of the tougher holes on the PGA Tour.

Glen Abbey Golf Club Oakville, Ontario				Hole	Yards	Par
	Length	Par	Rating	1	443	4
				2	414	4
Gold	7102	73	75.5	3	156	3
Blue	6618	73	72.5	4	417	4
White	6202	73	70.5	5	527	5
Yellow	5577	74	73.5	6	437	4
				7	197	3
				8	433	4
				9	458	4
				OUT	3482	35
				10	435	5
				11	452	4
				12	187	3
				13	529	5
				14	426	4
				15	141	3
				16	516	5
				17	434	4
				18	500	5
				IN	3620	38
				Total	7102	73

"fair shake" McIsaac pined for by acting as natural amphitheatres. "It is the best spectator course in the world," the designer said upon its completion in 1976. But it is the five holes along the creek, the "valley holes" kickstarted by a drive off the 11th tee into a gorge some 120 feet below, that burn themselves into the memories of competitors and spectators alike. These holes have the reputation of being one of the toughest stretches on the entire PGA Tour.

The 11th fairway, squeezed by trees on the left and bunkers on the right, ends abruptly. For at that point, Sixteen Mile Creek, ill-named because it is closer to a river in nature and has been known to tear out bridges when swollen by rain, flows across the hole. On the other side of the creek, the undulating green awaits, well bunkered and tucked in at the base of those towering bluffs. The waterway comes into play again on the par-three 12th, twice on the 13th (passing in front of the tee, continuing down the left boundary and then slicing back in front of the green, daring you to go for the long, narrow green in two shots) and on the par-four 14th, where it has claimed many a sliced drive. This has traditionally been one of the toughest holes on the course for the PGA Tour pros, with the stroke average approaching 4.5 some years. That average is inflated not only by the presence of the creek, but also by the swale that cuts through the centre of the rolling green, making three-putts commonplace.

While Glen Abbey can stretch up to 7,100 yards for the Canadian Open, the only PGA Tour event held outside the United States, a variety of tee positions offer distances right down to 5,200. "I regard the emphasis on length and huge greens as the two worst faults of modern golf course design," said Nicklaus. "Many people assume my golf courses will be long monsters, but I consider golf to be a game of precision, not strength." To his credit, Nicklaus kept in mind that the PGA Tour is at Glen Abbey for but one week each year. The rest of the 30,000 rounds are played by public golfers.

Nicklaus and Glen Abbey are linked in one more way, apparently for all time: Of all his Tour victories, 70 in total, none is a Canadian Open. He has been the runner-up an unbelievable seven times.

The slick greens at Glen Abbey, like the 12th, are among the best in the country.

From the fourteenth green, Glen Abbey ascends from the spectacular river valley.

How The Pros Play Glen Abbey

For Dave Barr, the veteran PGA Tour pro from British Columbia, one key to success at Glen Abbey is the left-to-right shot. Barr, who has finished as high as fourth in the Canadian Open here, believes the two toughest holes on the course are eight and nine. On the eighth, he tries to play down the left side beside the two bunkers, which leaves an open shot to the green with a long-iron. The key to the ninth, a long par-four, is keeping the ball in the fairway. "If you end up in the (right-side) bunker, you have to play a 210-yard sand shot," he said prior to the 1990 Open. Ironically, it was in that very situation that he found himself during the final round of the tournament. Taking only a minute amount of sand on the downswing with his two-iron meant a "fat" shot that found the pond some 50 yards short of the green. The resulting triple-bogey took him out of contention.

When he plays the Abbey, Barr believes he will score well if he can get through holes eight to 11 in even-par. The 13th hole, a 529-yard par-five, can be reached with two mighty blows. "I usually won't go for it unless I'm 220 yards or less from the green," says Barr, who has won more than $1 million on the pro tours.

On both 14, the 426-yard par-four, and 15, a par-three of 141 yards, the severe slope of the green means keeping the ball below the hole is a necessity. "The key to 16 is staying in the fairway," says Barr of the 516-yard par-five. "You can usually reach it in two from either side of the fairway. There's a good chance for a birdie here."

The 17th hole again favors a fade to stay away from the deep bunkers on the left. A good tee shot is rewarded with a short-iron approach. The 18th, a 500-yard par-five, has been called one of the great finishing holes. It tempts players to go for the green in two, but taunts them with a large pond in front of the long, narrow green. Three of the last six holes at the Abbey are par-fives, a situation that has made for some exciting conclusions to past Canadian Opens.

Greystone is one of the best new courses in Canada — but with a strong traditional feel.

GREYSTONE

Golf Club

Architect: Doug Carrick
Head Professional: Rick Sikorsky
General Manager: Irwin Blehm
Superintendent

The people behind Greystone spent several years seeking the ideal location for the culmination of their joint vision and finally found it in 230 acres at the base of the Niagara Escarpment west of Toronto. The philosophy behind the club states that it exists for "the pleasure of like-minded individuals with a true appreciation for the sport of golf."

In line with this theme, the founders selected a young Canadian architect with an innate sense of classic golf course design. Doug Carrick, responsible for other significant courses such as King Valley in Ontario, recalls the first time he walked the property. "The undulating terrain, the magnificent specimen trees, the dramatic elevation changes, the views of the escarpment and the surrounding countryside made me feel that the land offered great potential to create a golf course with a very special character.

"The course has been styled in the same fashion as some of the older classic layouts," says Carrick, "with modest-sized greens, steep-faced bunkers and plenty of undulations, emphasizing the need to develop one's shot-making ability.

"The first hole is a straightaway par 5 of 520 yards from an elevated tee to a slightly elevated green. Even though three bun-

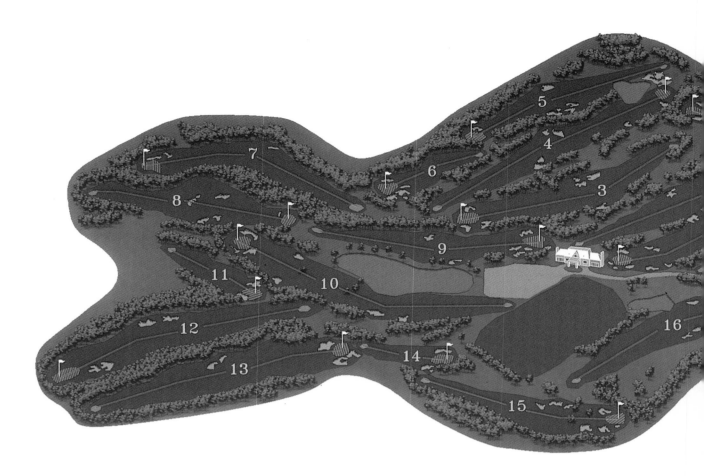

kers guard the fairway on the left and right sides of the landing area and three more guard the entrance to the green, the first hole allows the golfer a good chance to loosen up. The second hole is a strong par 3 of 202 yards that plays slightly uphill to an undulating green. The large specimen pine tree in the distance acts as a good target.

"The third is a demanding par 4 played from an elevated tee. A tee shot placed slightly right of centre will provide the best angle to approach the elevated green which is guarded left and right by three deep bunkers." Only the longest hitters will reach the fourth green in two shots. The gambler's tee shot must carry 230 yards over two bunkers, thus setting up the best approach. The more conservative golfer can play left off the tee, hitting his second and third shots to precise landing areas on the rolling, winding fairway. "The green is flanked on the left side by a large old abandoned sand pit which has been left in its natural state to give the hole a Scottish links character," Carrick says.

Number 5 is an outstanding par 4, featuring a tee shot from an elevated green to a landing area cut into a hillside and framed by four sculpted bunkers. Six is a classic par 3

with a deep swale angling from left to right in front of the green. Number 7 is the toughest hole on the course, says Carrick. (See sidebar)

The second shot on Number 8 must clear a deep ravine to a shallow green protected by a deep bunker on the left and large trees behind the green. The front nine concludes with a dogleg left par 4 which requires a long draw from the tee and then a mid-to-short iron approach to a narrow green surrounded by bumps, hollows and bunkers.

The 10th is a gambler's par 5, offering eagles, birdies — or double bogeys. Reaching the green in two is made even more hazardous by a deep ravine that slashes across in front of the green. A pond on the right side of the landing area combines with a plethora of bunkers and mounds to threaten wayward shots. Number 11 is an "enchanting" par 3, says Carrick, "carved through a beautiful mature woodlot of beech, maple, pine and birch." On 12, he says, "position off the tee is of primary importance as two bunkers cut into the hillside short of the green on the left will block out a drive played down the left side of the fairway." The 13th is a straightaway par 4, with the green and

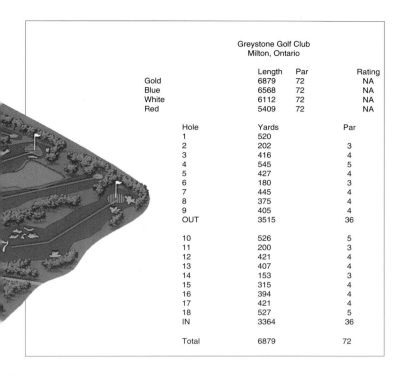

Greystone Golf Club Milton, Ontario			
	Length	Par	Rating
Gold	6879	72	NA
Blue	6568	72	NA
White	6112	72	NA
Red	5409	72	NA
Hole	Yards		Par
1	520		
2	202		3
3	416		4
4	545		5
5	427		4
6	180		3
7	445		4
8	375		4
9	405		4
OUT	3515		36
10	526		5
11	200		3
12	421		4
13	407		4
14	153		3
15	315		4
16	394		4
17	421		4
18	527		5
IN	3364		36
Total	6879		72

Trying to reach the par-5 10th in two shots is made more difficult by the ravine in front of the green.

The small 16th green demands a precise approach shot.

all the hazards visible from the tee. Although Number 14 is a short par 3, it places a premium on accuracy and club selection.

"The 15th hole is what I think will become known as the 'Greystone Hole,'" says Carrick, "as it plays into the dramatic backdrop of the Niagara Escarpment and is possibly the most attractive hole on the golf course. Measuring only 315 yards in length, it has a complex personality. The aggressive player can attempt to drive the green, setting up a birdie or eagle opportunity. However, triple bogeys on this hole are not out of the question."

On Number 16, a bold tee shot that carries four bunkers cut into the hillside on the right will leave a shorter shot into the green.

The 17th flows from right to left over rolling terrain and, again, the bunkers in the corner of the dogleg signal the best path to the shortest approach shot.

And of Number 18, Carrick says, "I wanted it to be a hole where the outcome of a match could be decided by bold and skilful shotmaking. It is reachable in two and allows for exciting eagle or birdie opportunities. With the tee shot ideally placed, the golfer must decide whether to play straight for the green over two bunkers jutting into the fairway from the right side or to lay up to the left side of the fairway, leaving a short pitch into the green. I think the variety of options available on Number 18 make it an exciting finishing hole."

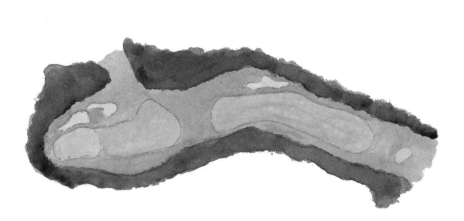

The Toughest Hole at Greystone

"At 445 yards from the back tees, Number 7 is perhaps the most difficult and dramatic hole on the golf course," says Greystone architect Doug Carrick. "The tee shot is played from a slightly elevated tee to a fairway that doglegs left through a beautiful stand of mature trees. A deep ravine flanks the left side of the fairway, running from the tee to the landing area and then sweeps across in front of the green. After a well-played tee shot down the middle of the fairway, the second shot must carry the valley to a dramatic hillside green protected on the right side by two bunkers. Two excellent shots will be required to set up a par or birdie on this hole. For the long-ball hitter, a second ledge has been sculpted into the hillside beyond the primary landing area to provide some incentive to cut the corner of the dogleg a little."

An abandoned sand pit flanks the 4th green at Greystone.

The East Course at Hamilton Golf and Country Club is the newest of the three nines, but is comparable to the original 18 in design and challenge.

—— *Ancaster, Ontario* ——

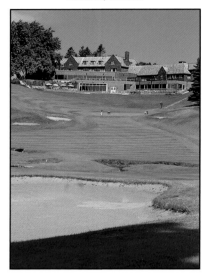

HAMILTON

Golf and Country Club

Architect: Harry Colt (18)
and C.E. Robinson (9)
Head Professional: Rob McDannold
Manager: John Mickle
Superintendent: Rod Trainor

Driving up to the stately, ivy-enveloped mansion which serves as the clubhouse for the Hamilton Golf and Country Club, even the most jaded golfer realizes that here is something extraordinary. The quiet, superlative elegance of both the course and the club is seldom matched anywhere in the world of golf.

The Hamilton Golf and Country Club was once located in the city of Hamilton, on the present site of the Hamilton Centre Mall, when it was founded in 1894. A couple of years later, yielding to the pressures of urban growth and accompanying tax pressures as many city courses did in those days, the club moved to acreage on the side of Hamilton Mountain. This location, now the Chedoke municipal course, served the membership until 1913 when the club's fathers decided to build 18 holes and an imposing clubhouse farther up the face of Hamilton Mountain, where the topography and view were unequalled.

Harry Colt, riding the success of his acclaimed new course at England's Sunningdale and the Toronto Golf Club, was contracted to design the layout. Drawing on his British heritage, he crafted a fine bump-and-run course which officially opened in 1916. At Sunningdale, Colt gave a hint of what would eventually be

one of his great contributions to golf course architecture: comprehensive tree-planting programs.

The site of Hamilton Golf and Country Club, which now covers more than 300 acres, was largely farmer's fields when the course was designed, a situation unimaginable to a present-day visitor. In the mind of present Head Professional Rob McDannold, Colt's visionary genius is unsurpassed: "When you look at the original map of this property, there were almost no trees. Now it looks as if it was carved out of the forest. Colt planned it so there are exact gaps in the trees for sunlight, for the wind, for shots. He had an absolutely amazing ability to foresee what this course would look like 50 years later. The trees look like they've been here forever."

An immediate success upon its opening, the Hamilton Golf and Country Club played host to the Canadian Open just three years later. The first national championship played after the end of the First World War, it drew more than usual interest for a number of reasons, not the least of which was the fact that it

Surrounded by forest and dotted with ponds and streams, Hamilton is a shotmaker's delight.

counted the great U.S. amateur Bobby Jones among the field. But Jones could do no better than a tie with Ottawa's Karl Keffer for second, as Douglas Edgar of Atlanta, Georgia, won the first of his two consecutive Open titles. Edgar's four-round total of 278 was at that time the world record for professionals. The second, and final, time the club opened its course to the Open, in 1930, Tommy Armour of Detroit defeated fellow PGA Tour pro Leo Diegel in a 36-hole playoff. To get into the playoff, Armour had to craft a stunning 64 in the final round, a course record at the time. Jim Nelford of Vancouver tied it in the 1977 Canadian Amateur, but still finished second to Rod Spittle. It has been recently broken by Warren Sye, who shot a stunning 62.

Playing the original 18 holes (the West and South nines) today can be very reminiscent of those early days when Jones and Armour trod Hamilton's fairways, for an astute membership has taken care to maintain the original design in large part. The rolling fairways are separated by those now-mature trees and the design is as valuable and serviceable as a fine

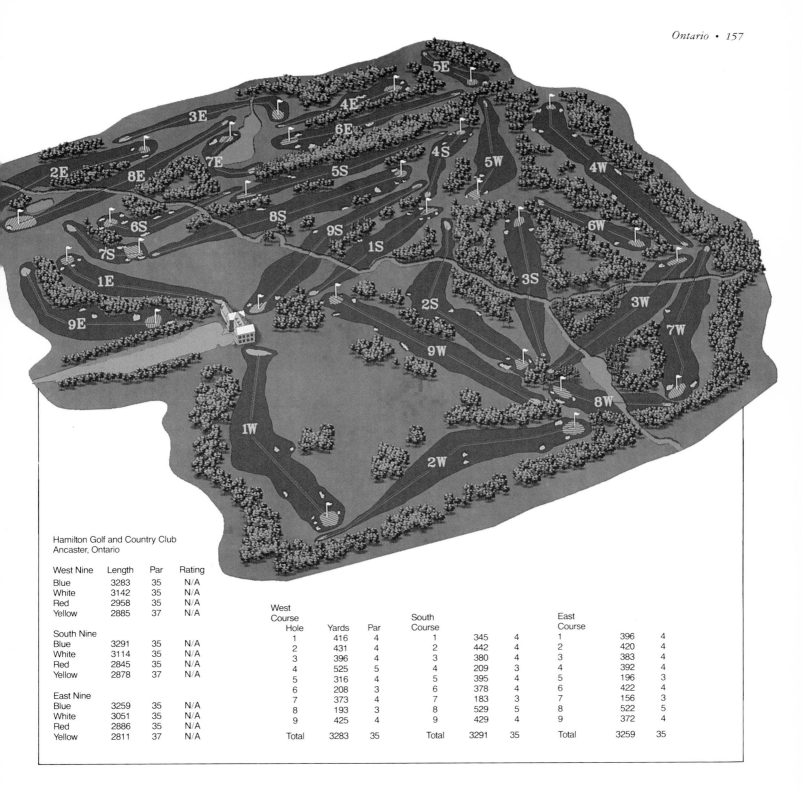

Hamilton Golf and Country Club
Ancaster, Ontario

West Nine	Length	Par	Rating
Blue	3283	35	N/A
White	3142	35	N/A
Red	2958	35	N/A
Yellow	2885	37	N/A

South Nine			
Blue	3291	35	N/A
White	3114	35	N/A
Red	2845	35	N/A
Yellow	2878	37	N/A

East Nine			
Blue	3259	35	N/A
White	3051	35	N/A
Red	2886	35	N/A
Yellow	2811	37	N/A

West Course Hole	Yards	Par	South Course			East Course		
1	416	4	1	345	4	1	396	4
2	431	4	2	442	4	2	420	4
3	396	4	3	380	4	3	383	4
4	525	5	4	209	3	4	392	4
5	316	4	5	395	4	5	196	3
6	208	3	6	378	4	6	422	4
7	373	4	7	183	3	7	156	3
8	193	3	8	529	5	8	522	5
9	425	4	9	429	4	9	372	4
Total	3283	35	Total	3291	35	Total	3259	35

antique. Colt, the first golf course architect who was not a professional golfer, nonetheless has managed to provide a fine test of golf. With only two par-fives, this beautifully conditioned 6,600-yard layout plays much longer than the card indicates.

While the course is not overly tight, well-positioned tee shots are vital to a respectable score. The majority of the par-fours require good planning and execution to prepare for the most advantageous approach to the green. Straying into the stands of mature hardwoods seldom means a lost ball, but those massive

trees will no doubt prevent advancing it once found. The par-threes at Hamilton are strong: all but one play to more than 180 yards from the blue tees and more than 175 from the whites.

"The first four holes can make or break you," says McDannold. "It's a very difficult start. The first two holes are par-fours of more than 400 yards. Your first drive has to be about 240 yards into the prevailing wind to the corner of the dogleg. You can't cut the corner, unless you can hit it at least 270, because the corner is filled with hills, valleys, pot bunkers and so on. So you have to play right, even though that gives you a longer shot in to a well-bunkered green. Number 2 is a dogleg-right, with bunkers right and trees left, that requires a long, accurate drive. The green has lots of bunkers and you're dealing with that wind again as you hit anything from a two- to a five-iron in.

"The third hole demands another accurate drive, but no more than 235 yards, otherwise you'll be down a steep slope covered with rough. Hit a long-iron off the tee, and you'll have about 165 in to an elevated green with a shelf. Don't be long on this one. The fourth hole can give you a bit of a reprieve if you hit it straight off the tee. In a tournament, I wouldn't hit driver off the tee here. There's a pit left, so stay a little right, but notice the trees and fairway bunkers down that side. This hole is reachable, but there's so many opportunities

The third hole on the West Course requires an iron off the tee and a mid-iron to hold the elevated green.

to get into trouble that I would just accept it being a three-shot hole and try to get close with that third shot. The green is long, narrow and elevated, bunkered left and front."

In 1975, the growing membership was placing an enormous burden on Colt's 18 holes, so the decision was made to bring in noted Canadian architect C.E. (Robbie) Robinson to design an additional nine holes of a complementary nature. "The East nine is spectacular," enthuses McDannold. "It's very tight; a great members' course."

It should be noted that Nicol Thompson, elder brother of talented course architect Stanley Thompson, served as the head professional at the Hamilton Golf and Country Club for 50 years until his retirement in 1945. He was succeeded by Dick Borthwick (1946-74), Ken Steeves (1975-80), Gary Maue (1981-89) and McDannold.

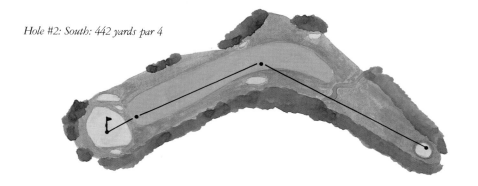

Hole #2: South: 442 yards par 4

The greens at Hamilton are not overly large, but are subtle and fast.

The Toughest Hole at Hamilton

"The second hole on our South course is the toughest of our 27," says Hamilton Head Professional Rob McDannold, "and I think it's one of the very best in Canada." Playing 442 yards from the blue tees and 406 from the whites, this hole demands a 230-yard drive to the corner of the dogleg-left. The mature stand of trees in the corner deters long-ball hitters from trying to carry the dogleg. McDannold suggests a three-wood off the tee, since a driver might carry the ball through the fairway. "From there, it's all uphill into the wind to an elevated green with a steep bunker right and trees, a slope and rough left," says the pro. "I tell most people to play up short of the green on their second shot and play it as a par-five; it saves them a lot of grief."

A reachable par-5, the fifth hole calls for a precise approach to the green.

KING VALLEY

Golf Club

Architect: Doug Carrick
Head Professional: Greg Shephard
Manager: Stan Waterhouse

King Valley is aptly named. Everything associated with it is regal, ranging from the awe-inspiring Tudor mansion which serves as an elegantly appointed clubhouse, to the equally impressive golf course which, although built in the early 1990s, has the look and feel of a mature classic.

Toronto's Doug Carrick, a very talented course architect with a instinctive feel for traditional design, was presented with an incredibly beautiful valley north of Toronto that cried out for a golf course: 165 acres of towering pines, majestic maples, beech and oaks, with tiny ponds dotting the undulating topography. The result harks back to the wonderful era of Canadian Stanley Thompson, Donald Ross and their colleagues 70 years ago,

It didn't take long for the King Valley course to gain a reputation for offering a memorable golf experience in a region of the country that is blessed with some of the best courses in the world. And when the owners, King Valley Development Corporation, constructed the stunningly opulent clubhouse, the legend of King Valley was complete.

Walking up the flagstone path leading to the clubhouse, it is almost impossible to believe that you are not approaching a historic English country manor. Its setting is breathtaking, framed

The 12th hole is a spectacular and challenging par 3.

		King Valley Golf Club King City, Ontario				
		Length	Par	Rating		
	Gold	6905	72	NA		
	Blue	6597	72	NA		
	White	6204	72	NA		
	Red	5552	73	NA		
Hole	Yards	Par				
1	408	4	10	372	4	
2	169	3	11	350	4	
3	409	4	12	217	3	
4	412	4	13	429	4	
5	501	5	14	505	5	
6	403	4	15	437	4	
7	199	3	16	166	3	
8	491	5	17	419	4	
9	433	4	18	585	5	
OUT	3425	36	IN	3480	3	
			Total	6905	72	

by wildflowers and stands of trees. The edifice (the mere word "building" does not convey its splendor) — complete with brick and limestone facade and wood shingles trimmed with copper flashing — is sculpted into the side of a ravine, offering commanding views of the ninth, 12th and 18th holes.

Every conceivable amenity is available to members of King Valley and their guests. Among those offered are valet parking and bag transportation, limousine service, a private study with complete secretarial services, specialty wine cellar and a billiards room.

No wonder that King Valley says that while "it is reserved for the select few, it will be the envy of many."

Obviously, no expense has been spared to make King Valley stand head and shoulders above its not inconsiderable competition. That is reinforced by the presence of Curtis Strange,

two-time winner of both the Canadian and U.S. Opens, on the club's marketing materials. Strange was retained by the owners as a design consultant and course advisor. "King Valley is a natural," says Strange. "It's a classic golfer's golf course set in a spectacular environment."

King Valley chose to offer transferable memberships, meaning that members who leave the club for whatever reason may sell, lease or otherwise transfer their memberships. The obvious advantage this plan has over traditional memberships is that the member doesn't lose his initiation fee should he have to leave the club.

While King Valley has retained the traditional values of the "Golden Age of Golf," Carrick has utilized all the modern-day innovations to provide the consummate golfing experience for those fortunate enough to play here. Aside from double-row irrigation,

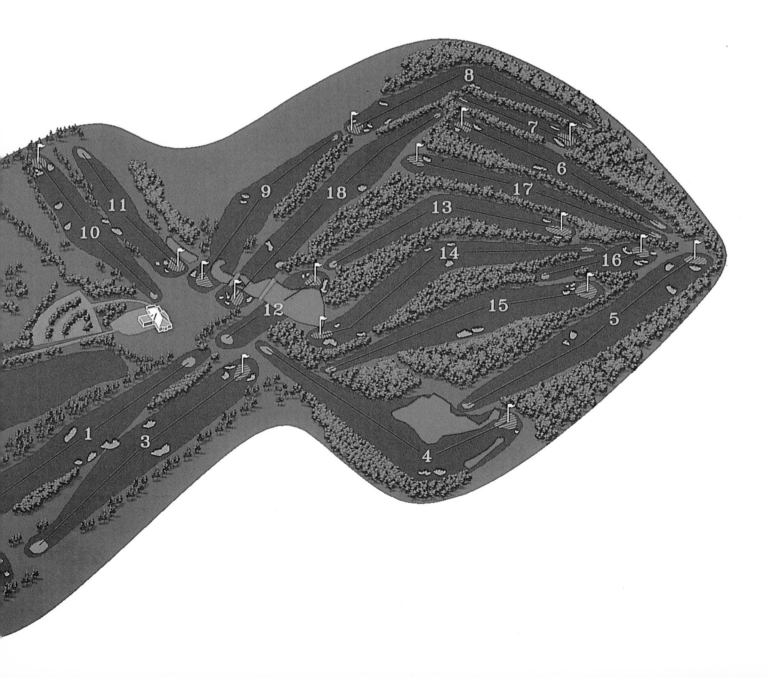

The Most Dangerous Hole at King Valley

Termed the "most dangerous hole" in King Valley's excellent course narrative, the 412-yard fourth is a spectacular par 4 played from an elevated tee. It is a dogleg left which curls around a large pond which extends all the way to the green. A long, straight

tee shot placed as close to the pond as you dare leaves a short iron to a narrow green. A pond lurks on the right side of the green, creating an island effect. A narrow neck of fairway leads into the green for the more cautious player who may wish to run the ball up, since an approach which goes long will end up in a bunker in the back right corner.

Number 14 is an outstanding double-dogleg par 5.

*King Valley's 18th is a fine finishing hole
with a pond in front of the green.*

Ohio bunker sand and splendid bentgrass playing surfaces, there is a six-acre multi-featured practice facility complete with bentgrass tees, target greens, putting and chipping greens with a variety of grassy hollows and mounds as well as two practice bunkers.

The design of the course itself is superbly well-balanced, with a par of 36 on each nine, consisting of four par 3s, 10 par 4s and four par 5s of varying lengths. Expect to use every club in your bag and to be tested for length, accuracy and finesse.

Aside from the par-4 fourth (see sidebar), King Valley's hole-by-hole narrative identifies Numbers 8, 9 and 18 as "signature holes".

The eighth hole, a 491-yard par 5 from the back tees, is a dogleg left through a spruce and pine plantation on the first portion of the fairway and then through a hardwood bush on the second. The ideal tee shot must carry 250 yards over a bunker in the corner of the dogleg. The second shot is then played across a small valley and stream, rising back up the hill to an elevated, tilted green guarded by three steep-faced bunkers and out of bounds on the right.

The subsequent hole is an exhilarating downhill par 4, with the tee situated at the highest point of the course and offering tremendous views of the surrounding countryside. A long tee shot down the right side leaves the best approach onto the green with a middle iron. The undulating green is protected on the right by a menacing bunker and a pond on the left front. Avoid being above the hole.

Your round at King Valley concludes with a spectacular par 5 sprawling 585 yards down a slope to a green severed from the fairway by a pond. The tee shot is played from a slightly elevated tee to the fairway which is canted from right to left. One bunker on the left and grassy hollows on the right cut into the hillside to protect the first landing area. The second shot must be placed beyond a bunker flanking the right side of the second landing area, setting up a short iron approach across the pond onto the angled green. A bunker on the front left of the green combine with three more to the right and rear to add to the unique challenge of King Valley's final hole.

Walking off the 18th green, gazing up at the imposing yet hospitable clubhouse, you will concur with Curtis Strange, who says: "I have gone around my share of golf courses in my career as a golf professional. The King Valley course is very special — a natural, and destined to become a classic."

*Extensive water, mounding and bunkering,
indicate your strategy at Lionhead.*

— *Brampton, Ontario* —

LIONHEAD

Golf and Country Club

Architect: *Ted Baker*
Head Professional: *Chuck Lorimer*
General Manager: *Alan Ogilvie*
Superintendent: *Jim Molenhuis*

Lionhead roared into existence in 1991, calling itself "the most 'private' public golf facility in Canada," and it has never looked back. Its stated goal was to provide a golfing experience for the public that previously had been available only at the best private clubs. Many knowledgeable observers feel it attained that goal almost from the day the doors opened.

"Lionhead has the fastest greens outside of the Masters tournament itself," said PGA Tour pro Dave Barr after winning the nationally televised 1991 Cadillac Classic skins game at Lionhead. "The Legends nine could very well become the most famous nine holes of golf in the world," echoed 1991 British Open winner Ian Baker-Finch after an outing at the then 27-hole facility. (Lionhead expanded to 36 holes early in the 1993 season.)

Like these players, golf writers tend to rave over the stunning layout that crisscrosses a river valley just outside Brampton. "Lionhead is a gem to watch for in the world's top 100," predicted the Toronto Star. Golf Digest said it was "one of the best courses, public or private, to be found anywhere."

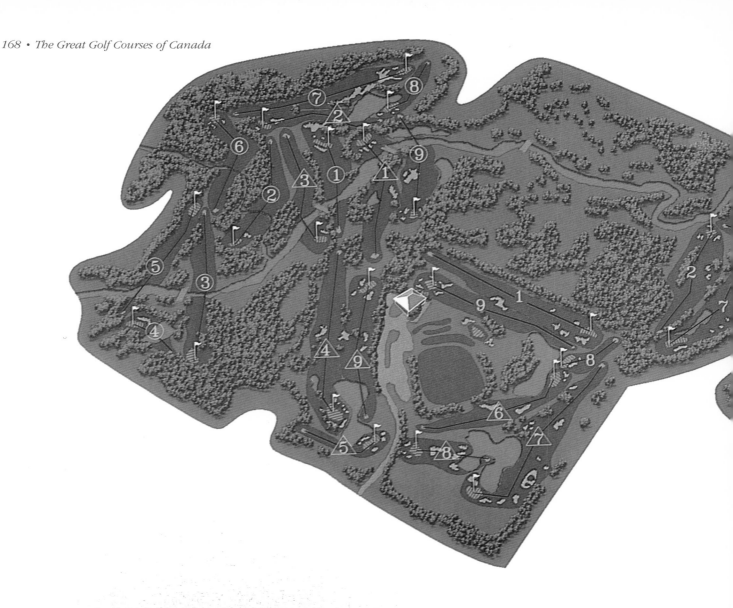

Those comments are music to the ears of the force behind Lionhead, Ignat (Iggy) Kaneff, president of Kaneff Properties Ltd. "We want to be recognized as the best golf facility in Canada," he said when Lionhead opened.

"Our immediate goal is to become the top-ranked course in Canada," says head professional Chuck Lorimer. "We're simply approaching it in a different way. We want to be thought of as a special event, much like attending a Blue Jays game or going to the Molson Indy. Everything we do here is first-class and I believe our reputation is becoming an incentive for people to want to come here. It's not inexpensive, but it's good value for your entertainment dollar.

"One of our major targets is corporate entertainment. What could be better than entertaining clients at a golf course that has an elegant atmosphere? We put great emphasis on service. All our employees take special seminars that make them sensitive to our customers' every need. We make people want to come back to Lionhead —

not just because we have a fabulous golf course, but because they are treated royally."

The royal treatment, akin to that at elite private clubs, begins when you turn off Mississauga Road about five kilometres north of Highway 401 into Lionhead's entrance. An attendant in the gatehouse bids you to stop, checks to ensure you have a tee time and then welcomes you. As you pull into the parking lot, a valet comes to get your bag and chauffeur you to the 40,000-square-foot clubhouse.

The clubhouse is the hub of Lionhead and was designed to ensure every golfer, whether part of a corporate outing or out as a single, is treated as a pampered guest. Four locker rooms, five dining rooms, three lounges and an excellent pro shop, all served by courteous staff, provide enough amenities for even the most demanding customer.

After checking in at the clubhouse, the visitor walks 100 yards to one of the best practice facilities at any club, private or public. Covering almost three acres, it fea-

Lionhead Golf & Country Club
Brampton, Ontario

Legend/Champion Courses

	Length	Par	Rating
Black	7200	72	77
Gold	6846	72	75
White	6439	72	73.2
Red	5833	72	70.1

Legend Course			Masters Course		
Hole	Yards	Par			
1	378	4	1	515	5
2	436	4	2	399	4
3	563	5	3	166	3
4	143	3	4	411	4
5	426	4	5	437	4
6	395	4	6	558	5
7	580	5	7	408	4
8	200	3	8	176	3
9	426	4	9	435	4
Total	3547	36	Total	3505	36

Champion Course		
1	458	4
2	432	4
3	454	4
4	539	5
5	189	3
6	415	4
7	530	5
8	193	3
9	443	4
Total	3653	36

Lionhead's dual personality: a view from the tablelands down to the river valley.

tures turf tees, two large putting and chipping greens, and a practice bunker.

The course at Lionhead built its reputation on 27 holes, composed of three very different nines: the Masters, Legends and Champions. Each played to a par of 36 and each was about 3,600 yards from the back tees.

The Masters featured forests, wooded ravines and steeply rolling terrain demanding

strategic play. The Legends was located in a valley crossing the Credit River four times, with wetlands, ponds and woods coming into play. The Champions opened with a truly spectacular first tee perched high on the bluffs, hitting down into the valley. Two other holes were played on river meadows before heading up to the tablelands with their earthen berms and ponds.

Open to the public, Lionhead's conditioning challenges that of the best private courses.

Lionhead Hosts Skins Tournament

Veteran PGA Tour pro Dave Barr from Richmond, B.C., made the best of the Cadillac Classic skins tournament held in Canada from 1989 through 1991, collecting a total of $299,00 while winning all three events. In the final edition,

held at Lionhead in August 1991, Barr gave an early indication of what was to come, landing his approach shot on the first hole less than an inch from the cup. Unfortunately, Fuzzy Zoeller also made a birdie and the money carried over to the third hole, a par 5 where Fuzzy made another birdie for $15,000. Arnold Palmer chipped in on the sixth for $10,000. Peter Jacobsen's par on the ninth was worth $20,000. On the back nine, Barr birdied the 10th, 12th, 13th and 15th holes. All but the one on 13 were for skins which brought his total to $85,000. Jacobsen (shown at right) collected $15,000 with an eagle on 16 and Barr's two-foot putt on 18 lipped out to give Zoeller $50,000

However, as previously mentioned, Lionhead is nothing if not forward looking. As of mid-1993, a new nine will be complete and the entire course will be realigned into two 18s: the Masters and the Legends. The Masters, an "Arizona-style layout" according to Lorimer, will feature moguls and mounding on the tablelands above the river valley. It will incorporate the existing Masters nine, three new holes and holes 4 to 9 of the old Champions. The new Legends will be an extremely impressive championship layout, located entirely in the valley. It will be comprised of three holes of the old Champions, six new holes and the existing Legends nine.

The presence of the Credit River gives the magnificently difficult Legends its diabolical character. Water figured into the design of every single hole on the old Legends nine.

However, the proximity of the river and its integration into the course design posed significant challenges for the developers and architect Ted Baker. No less than one year of study of the fauna and flora was required. Working closely with the Credit Valley Conservation Authority, many of the trees were preserved with careful planning and one Manitoba maple, unique to the property, was saved by constructing an island in the centre of one of the main irrigation ponds.

"Great care has been taken to preserve the natural beauty of the meadows, forests and natural foliage of the land on which Lionhead has been developed," Kaneff explains.

One would expect nothing less from Lionhead and its impressive people, no more than anyone doubts their sincere desire to become "the finest golf facility in Canada."

MAD RIVER

Golf Club

Architect: Bob Cupp
Head Professional: Gary Slatter
Superintendent/Manager: Ray Richards

After a roller-coaster drive through the camelbacked Hockley Hills northwest of Toronto, the sight of the stone pillars marking the entrance to Mad River Golf Club comes as a blessed relief. The driveway winds past the practice range before you see the club-house, which resembles nothing more than an oversized Victorian farmhouse of blue-grey clapboard.

The clubhouse says much about the Mad River philosophy. It is unpretentious, but exquisite in design and detail — much like the course itself. And as proud as the members and staff are of the facility, they are quick to point out that there is much more to Mad River than just a golf course; Mad River prides itself on its "values."

Head professional Gary Slatter explains: "The way Mad River Golf Club officially opened is a prime example of our values here. The opening tournament was a scramble and on every team was a beginner, an experienced player and two golfers of average ability. One of the women said she had been a member of another club for eight years and had never participated in an event, because she had never been encouraged to. She has played here ever since and loves the game."

Mad River, an equity membership club open to only 300 members, is smack in the middle of Central Ontario's ski country and provides chalet owners with a very worthwhile excuse to head north during the summer months. As reflected by the clubhouse and setting, the atmosphere is casual, appropriate for vacationers and cottagers. There is only one rule at Mad River, says Slatter: No smoking in the clubhouse. There is not even a dress code!

"Our values — not rules — allow the professional to talk to any player who is truly outlandish but in two years it has not been a problem," Slatter says. "And our juniors look like juniors, not like little PGA Tour pros. We have no tee times and no restrictions. A junior beginner has the same opportunities as the chairman of the board. We have guest days, not women's guest days and men's guest days."

Course architect Bob Cupp recognized the Mad River credo when designing the course. "The playability of Mad River is intended to cover the breadth of playing ability. The design maximizes the natural qualities of the land: beautiful long views, a mixture of open and treed areas, a wide variety of mature

The Mad River course heads into the trees on Number 12: safe players go right, bold left.

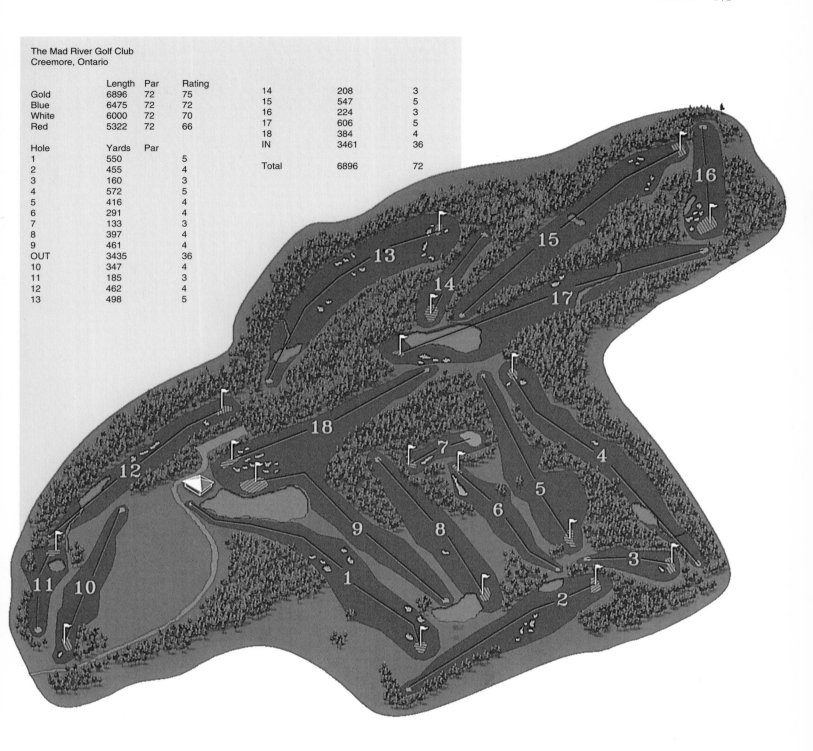

The Mad River Golf Club
Creemore, Ontario

	Length	Par	Rating
Gold	6896	72	75
Blue	6475	72	72
White	6000	72	70
Red	5322	72	66

Hole	Yards	Par
1	550	5
2	455	4
3	160	3
4	572	5
5	416	4
6	291	4
7	133	3
8	397	4
9	461	4
OUT	3435	36
10	347	4
11	185	3
12	462	4
13	498	5
14	208	3
15	547	5
16	224	3
17	606	5
18	384	4
IN	3461	36
Total	6896	72

hardwood and pine. It utilizes a high-quality, two-shot strategy, offering optional difficult challenges with commensurate rewards.

"The most striking and memorable element of the course design, however, is the shadows. The land is a series of substantial mounds of small ridges that provide excellent counterslopes, resulting in superb golf. The ridges, some as high as 100 feet, offer a myriad of interesting golf presentations. The green areas are shaped to provide run-up shots and high-quality chipping — a quality

all but forgotten by modern designers. There is always an entrance to the green which will accommodate a rolling approach — though it may not always end up near the pin.

"The relative length of the shots is not intended to be equal on each hole," cautions Cupp. "The idea is not for each player to experience a driver and five-iron from their respective tees. In some cases, the contour of this wonderful property may cause tees to be placed in locations where, from one set of tees, a driver and a wedge may be required, and, from the next set forward or back, a driver and a three-iron may be needed.

"There are also great ranges of lengths of each par. There are long, medium and short par 3s, 4s and 5s. It's also important to note that each green has at least one completely open pin location and at least one tucked away. This is the mechanism that changes the course's personality the most (other than the weather).

"There are also a fairly even number of turns (doglegs) to the right and left on the par 4s and 5s, and a very definite intent to place holes of certain length into or with prevailing northwest winds with consideration to occasional north winds," Cupp explains. "The directions of the par 3s and par 5s cover every point of the compass. They are excellently matched as to length, slope and difficulty.

"The ultimate goal is to provide fun golf for a large variety of talents in a beautifully unique and exclusive setting," the architect concludes.

There is no question that Cupp, and the founders of Mad River, have attained that goal in admirable fashion.

The 16th tee offers a great view of the finishing holes at Mad River.

Number 13 represents one of the most striking tee shots at Mad River.

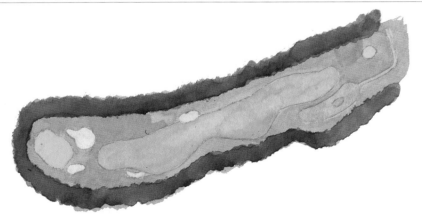

The Toughest Hole at Mad River

Gary Slatter, head professional at Mad River Golf Club, says the toughest hole has proven to be the fourth, a par 5 of 572 yards from the gold tees, 550 from the blues, 528 from the whites or 476 from the red blocks. "The drive must be straight to avoid dense, unforgiving forest on the right and a pond and more forest on the left. The second shot must also be accurate, as the forest continues down both sides of the fairway, and there is a target trap on the right. A great second shot can get a player past the 150-yard marker. However, the third shot is to an island green, surrounded not by water, but by severe slopes left and behind, as well as bunkers guarded both sides at the front. The safest place to miss the third shot is short or possibly right where a deep grass hollow allows a reasonable up-and-down opportunity. A par 5 on this hole is exceptional, a double bogey average."

Mandarin is a picturesque members' course, as epitomized by the par-3 16th hole.

MANDARIN

Golf and Country Club

Architect: Doug Carrick
Director of Golf: Matthew Yustin
Manager: Steve Lam
Superintendent: John Cunningham

One of the new breed of equity golf clubs, Mandarin Golf and Country Club northeast of Toronto called upon one of the new breed on the PGA Tour to give it a hand.

Steve Jones, winner of the 1989 Canadian Open, was enlisted as the design consultant to architect Doug Carrick of Toronto. The input of a Tour player is no doubt of value, and Jones is quick to compliment everyone else associated with this facility.

"The renowned architectural firm of Robinson, Carrick Associates Ltd. has been responsible for some of this country's most prestigious and challenging courses," says Jones. "They have created this unique course which offers its members and guests some challenging and memorable holes.

Mandarin, an extension of the Mandarin Club of Toronto, is the brainchild of four Hong Kong-born businessmen, all of whom have been based in Canada for almost 20 years: Herbert Chang, Henry Hung, Joseph Au-yeung and Stephen Wong. The present layout, which opened in 1991, has risen from the ashes of a previous 27-hole facility.

"Basically, we tore apart the whole course and started from scratch," says Carrick. "A lot of work and thought has gone into the

The pretty par-3 8th hole at Mandarin.

The Mandarin Golf & Country Club
Unionville, Ontario

	Length	Par	Rating
Blue	6565	71	72.1
White	6108	71	69.8
Red	5182	71	65.2

Hole	Yards	Par
1	553	5
2	384	4
3	194	3
4	417	4
5	522	5
6	169	3
7	419	4
8	150	3
9	368	4
OUT	3176	35
10	532	5
11	379	4
12	455	4
13	353	4
14	166	3
15	400	4
16	155	3
17	423	4
18	526	5
IN	3389	36
Total	6565	71

project and it has become an outstanding course. Our objective is to provide our clients with a successful and profitable golf facility of lasting character and beauty, that will provide challenge and enjoyment for golfers of all skill levels for years to come."

Carrick describes Mandarin as a "modernized version of the old classic style of golf courses built in the 1920s and '30s. Modest-sized, gently rolling greens surrounded by flowing, sculpted bunkers set the framework for the course. Generous fairways defined by strategic bunkering and open green entrances provide challenge and interest for the expert player, yet offer a very playable and enjoyable experience for the majority of members."

At just over 6,500 yards from the championship tees, Mandarin is not excessively long by modern standards. However, it demands accurate, well-placed tee shots, precise iron play and strategic planning in order to score well. Water comes into play on 10 holes and more than 80 bunkers add to the challenge

and aesthetic appeal of the course. More than 225,000 cubic yards of earth were moved and in excess of 700 mature trees added in order to create a course with immediate character and maturity.

The first hole, a 547-yard par 5 dogleg, plays slightly uphill from the tee and then down to the green. Use the bunkers in each landing area as your directional guides. Number 2 is a relatively short downhill par 4 which calls for an approach shot of 130 to 140 yards to a green flanked by water on the left. A stone wall accents the back left pin placement adjacent to the water. The third hole is a 197-yard par 3 with four bunkers guarding the green.

Long hitters have a chance of reaching the 513-yard fifth hole in two, provided they avoid the trees and out-of- bounds guarding the entire right side of the fairway. The green is nestled in a grove of trees, with a bunker lurking on the left. The par-3 sixth hole requires a long iron across water to a green angled from left to right. Number 7 is a

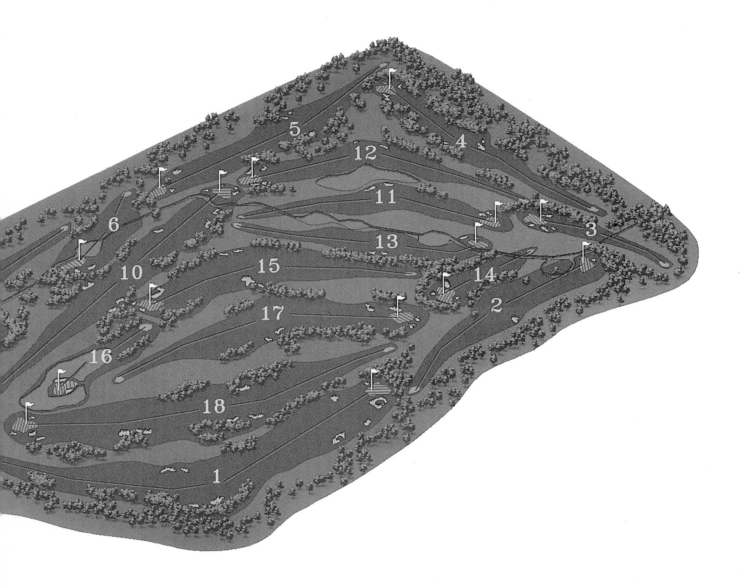

To birdie Number 5, you must avoid trees and out of bounds on the right side.

straightaway par 4 of 394 yards with a stream running down the entire left side of the fairway and crossing in front of the green. The trees and out-of-bounds on the right side of this hole add to its challenge.

You will have noted the par-3 eighth hole on your way into the club. This picturesque hole requires a precise mid-iron to avoid the pond on the left and bunkers on the right and left. Water crosses in front of the ninth tee at about 160 yards out and then heads down the right side of the fairway to the green.

The 525-yard 10th hole challenges players to try to hit the green in two. Adding to the player's dilemma is the creek that crosses immediately in front of the green. Number 11 is a sweeping dogleg par 4 of 383 yards.

The drive must skirt the trees on the right to set up the best angle of approach to the well-bunkered green. The 12th hole is a long par 4 which is draped around a large pond. Two fairway bunkers guard the right side, making length and accuracy a must. The long narrow green is protected by three bunkers, making this hole the toughest on the course.

The 13th is a short but tricky par 4 of 339 yards. A series of ponds and a stream flank the left side of the fairway for its entire length before crossing in front of the green. Two bunkers on the right side of the fairway combine with the stream on the left to demand a very accurate drive. A good tee shot sets up a wedge approach to the shallow angled green guarded by water and bunkers. Number 14 is a medium-length uphill par 3 to a green protected by four bunkers.

The drive on the par-4 15th must carry a bunker on the left corner of the dogleg, leaving the best approach to the green which is angled from left to right. Sixteen is the feature hole at Mandarin (see sidebar). Mandarin's finishing holes provide an exciting climax to a round. The 17th is a strong par 4 with a gentle dogleg right. Three bunkers sit on the right side of the fairway while three others protect the green. At 525 yards, the 18th is reachable in two, but the approach shot must avoid water on the right side of the green as well as several bunkers on the left side.

Dependent on membership sales (approximately 500 will be sold), plans call for an indoor swimming pool with retractable roof, indoor and outdoor tennis courts, squash court, badminton court, indoor driving range and a multi-dimensional outdoor practice facility.

"Our plan," says Chang, "is to provide our members with much more than golf. We want an outstanding facility which can be used 12 months a year." The proposed three-storey clubhouse would cover almost 50,000 square feet and, in addition to the sports facilities, would include a dining room specializing in haute Chinese cuisine, a lounge and poolside cafe.

The Signature Hole at Mandarin Golf and Country Club

Course architect Doug Carrick calls Number 16 the "feature hole at Mandarin. Measuring only 169 yards, the tee shot is played across water to a small island green guarded by two bunkers. The pond and greens on the 16th and 18th holes provide a centrepiece for viewing these two holes from the clubhouse."

The scenic Credit River winds its way through the heart of the Mississaugua Golf and Country Club.

MISSISSAUGUA

Golf and Country Club

Architect: George Cumming
Head Professional: Gar Hamilton
Manager: Walter Haselsteiner
Superintendent: Paul White

Rarely in the course of any human endeavor is there one such single symbolic moment as is evident in the founding of the Mississaugua Golf and Country Club.

As recounted in the club's history, written to salute its 75th anniversary in 1981, the scene was set when a group of enthusiastic members of the Highlands Golf Club, which was about to fall victim to development, were travelling in a surrey down a dirt road which paralleled the Credit River west of Toronto. It was the autumn of 1905 and their mission was to find a new golfing home well removed from the city.

"The day was warm and the road was dusty," the chronicle notes. "When the men spotted a couple of fruit trees, they halted the surrey to pick some apples. On impulse, John Hall jumped a low fence and strode across a broad meadow. He gazed in astonishment at the beautiful scene down the valley, then turned to his friends and shouted, 'We've found it!'

" 'Found what?' they shouted back. 'Why, our golf course, of course!' Hall replied.

"Hall returned to the surrey and, impulsively pulling a golf club from his bag, picked up a ball and went back to the top of the

The 417-yard par four 8th hole features a tight green protected by sand and trees.

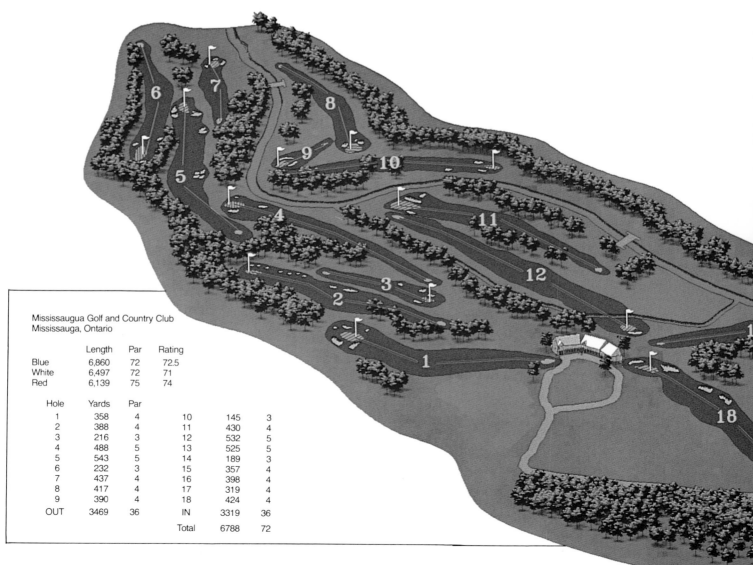

Mississaugua Golf and Country Club
Mississauga, Ontario

	Length	Par	Rating
Blue	6,860	72	72.5
White	6,497	72	71
Red	6,139	75	74

Hole	Yards	Par			
1	358	4	10	145	3
2	388	4	11	430	4
3	216	3	12	532	5
4	488	5	13	525	5
5	543	5	14	189	3
6	232	3	15	357	4
7	437	4	16	398	4
8	417	4	17	319	4
9	390	4	18	424	4
OUT	3469	36	IN	3319	36
			Total	6788	72

hill. He teed up, swung his brassie and drove the ball far into the valley below."

With such fervor, moulded in the heat generated by the discovery of such an awesome setting, the founders overlooked such picayune details as the fact that the course was all but inaccessible to the transportation modes of that era and that a wealthy, enthusiastic membership had to be raised. All such apparent obstacles were successfully dealt with in turn.

The club was extremely fortunate in having as its first president, Lauchlan Alexander Hamilton, land commissioner of the Canadian Pacific Railway. Among his feats was the surveying and laying out of the city of Vancouver. The club archives make this assessment: "He laid out the City of Vancouver and then devoted the rest of his career to the making of the Mississaugua Golf Club." Hamilton was president for 10 years and, by the time he retired, the lovely Tudor-style clubhouse had been completed and the club was settled and prosperous.

George Cumming, the noted professional at the Toronto Golf Club and 1905 Canadian Open champion, was responsible for Mississaugua's initial layout in 1906 with the assistance of Percy Barrett, professional at Toronto's Lambton club. In 1909, Cumming was commissioned to revamp the course. Famed architect Donald Ross of Dornoch, Scotland, and Pinehurst, North Carolina, toured the course 10 years later, making recommendations to change bunkering and lengthen holes. Thus, by 1923, the course had been all but rebuilt. Apart from changes in 1928, 1958 and the late 1980s, the course has not changed sub-

stantially since. From its opening holes on the bluffs overlooking the serpentine Credit River, it swoops down into the valley where John Hall drove his ball in 1905. Snaking along the valley, it loops back and forth across the river before wending its way back up the precipitous bank.

Mississaugua's physical attributes are as enviable as the unequalled calibre of its membership. In its early years, it was home to "Canada's premier golfing family" — the Thompson brothers. Bill, Stanley and Frank were the Mississaugua contingent of the five brothers. Nicol was the eldest, a professional who played out of the Hamilton Golf and Country Club in nearby Ancaster, Ontario. Matt lived and worked in the golf trade in Manitoba. The first record of their achievements came in 1919 when the three amateurs finished one, two and three in the first Toronto and District Golf Tournament to be held after the war. Frank and Bill went on to capture many tournaments including national amateur titles. Stanley, while a formidable player, would make his mark as one of the most esteemed golf course architects in the world. Indeed, he would redesign and lengthen the Mississaugua course in later years.

Although several Toronto-area courses can make a legitimate claim to Ada Mackenzie, this Canadian golfing legend took up the game by hitting balls at the Mississaugua course at the age of 17. Both during and after her time at Mississaugua, she would make an indelible mark on the game in this country, leading to her induction into the Canadian Golf Hall of Fame. When she died in 1973 at the age of 81, Ada Mackenzie had won almost every major tournament at home and abroad, including five Canadian Ladies' Opens and five Canadian Close championships, eight Canadian Ladies' Seniors Golf Association Championships and two Ontario Seniors titles. In 1933, she won every major ladies' golf championship in Canada and was named the outstanding female athlete in the country.

Tradition is a Mississaugua byword, and no mention of the club would be complete without discussing the contribution of Gordon Brydson, head professional from 1932 to 1971 and an honorary life member since. He was a fine tournament player, winning the Canadian PGA Championship, two Ontario Opens and the Quebec Open, but it is for his unstinting contribution to the life of "his" club that he is revered. "Mississaugua has been my second home," he has said. And the sentiment is reciprocated, as one longtime member stated

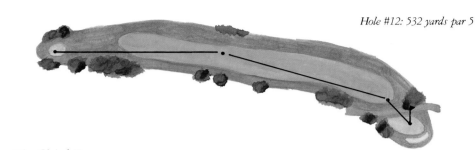

Hole #12: 532 yards par 5

The Big Chief Factor

In addition to numerous other tournaments, Mississaugua Golf and Country Club has played host to six Canadian Open Championships: 1931 (Walter Hagen), 1938 (Sam Snead), 1942 (Craig Wood), 1951 (Jim Ferrier), 1965 (Gene Littler) and 1974 (Bobby Nichols). It is safe to say that in every tournament round, the par-five 12th hole, nicknamed the Big Chief, has played a role. It was the site of spectacular play in 1938 during a playoff between eventual winner Sam Snead and Harry Cooper. Snead's second shot was a five-wood which hit a spectator and bounced onto the green, 35 feet from the hole. Cooper was off the green in two and chipped to 25 feet. Snead, trailing by one shot, putted for his eagle while Cooper rolled in the birdie putt. In 1965, Jack Nicklaus came to grief on this hole when his second shot cleared the river, but came to rest on the side of the plateau on which the green sits. Carding a bogey instead of an eagle or even birdie or par, it has been said, "cost Nicklaus the Open." He lost to Gene Littler by one shot in what might have been considered an omen. Of all his titles, the Canadian Open eluded Nicklaus for his entire career.

More cautious players lay up in front of the river with their second shot on the par-five 13th.

at Brydson's 80th birthday party in 1987: "Gordie has been Mississaugua; that's all there is to it."

Present Head Professional Gar Hamilton, an ideal successor to Brydson in many aspects, says Mississaugua is "an outstanding old course that is often underrated." He points to back-to-back par-fives on the back nine that typify the course's toughness.

"This course is very difficult," says Hamilton, "because it never lets up; it's relentless. The middle of the course is key to a good scoring round. Number 12 is an old hole, the par-five Big Chief. The temptation there is to go for the green in two, but you've got to hit your second shot to a small, elevated green over the river. Not a high-percentage shot for most players . . .

"The 13th is a very difficult par-five as well. The fairway slopes quite a bit, leaving a small landing area if you want to try to get home with two shots. You'll need two absolutely perfect shots to get home here; anything less leaves you with a poor lie. In fact, many players lay up in front of the river on their second shot, just to make sure."

By the way, if you're wondering why the golf club's name is spelled differently than the city's name, there's no good reason, says the club's history. In the 1940s, "the club changed the spelling of its name from Mississauga (which corresponded with both the name of the Mississauga Indians, whose heritage was associated with the land, and the club's address on Mississauga Road) to Mississaugua, which corresponds, historically, with nothing at all." No one has been able to determine the logic behind the change in the years since.

No. 10, a short par-three, requires hitting over the Credit River, a recurring hazard at Mississaugua.

A small lake guards the 17th and 18th fairways, making the National's finishing holes among the most difficult in Canada.

Woodbridge, Ontario

THE NATIONAL

Golf Club

Architects: Tom and George Fazio
Director of Golf: Ben Kern
Superintendent: John Cherry

The National. To those who know this course, consistently rated the toughest in Canada, no two words inspire the same respect or, in some cases, fear.

The National Golf Club was opened in 1974, the culmination of a dream held by businessman Gil Blechman. "I wanted to build the best course in the world; a U.S. Open-type course," Blechman says. He enlisted Tom and George Fazio, two of the world's premier course architects, to build the best possible layout on the 400 acres he had assembled in the rolling hills north of Woodbridge, Ontario.

They were more than equal to the task. Lee Trevino, who won the 1979 Canadian Professional Golfers' Association Championship here, still calls it one of his favorite courses in the world. It is a note of distinction for The National that Trevino's winning score was 285 — one over par. Perhaps the one true mark of a great course is that it is never humbled; not even by the best.

"Everyone always talks about how difficult and hard the golf course is," says Blechman, who sold the course to the members in 1987, "but it is only the odd person who really appreciates its terrible beauty. You literally get seduced going around the bend from No. 10 to No. 13, and it's continually building to a crescendo until you come to 17 and 18."

It has been said that the first three holes of The National lure the unwary, the unprepared and the high-handicapper into a false sense of security. The opening tee shot is invited down a comfortingly sloped fairway; if you stay slightly left off the tee, hitting the well-protected green should be only a short-iron situation. The second hole is a straightaway par-four, and the third another downhill par-four with an emphasis on the second shot into a green guarded on the left by a pond and on the right by bunkers. The good player may well be at even par when stepping onto the fourth tee. A humbling experience awaits.

The fourth hole is the toughest on the course, a tortuous par-five that may send the wayward hitter to the fifth tee smarting from a double-bogey. And that is just a glimpse of what lies ahead. The next hole, the first par-three you encounter, is 180 yards from the blue tees, generally into the wind to a green encircled by bunkers. Err to the left, since a slice will route your ball down a hillside and onto the fourth fairway.

As windswept and open as the front nine may be, the trip home is shorter, narrower, heavily wooded, and sports water in play on all nine holes. A river valley some 100 feet lower than the front nine provides the routing for some of the most difficult holes in Canada. Your initiation to the back nine is dramatic. The tee for the par-three 10th hole is high on a bluff, while the green awaits in the valley far below. Club selection and a smooth swing are vital here, since danger lurks in the form of rough in front, a pond right and a huge

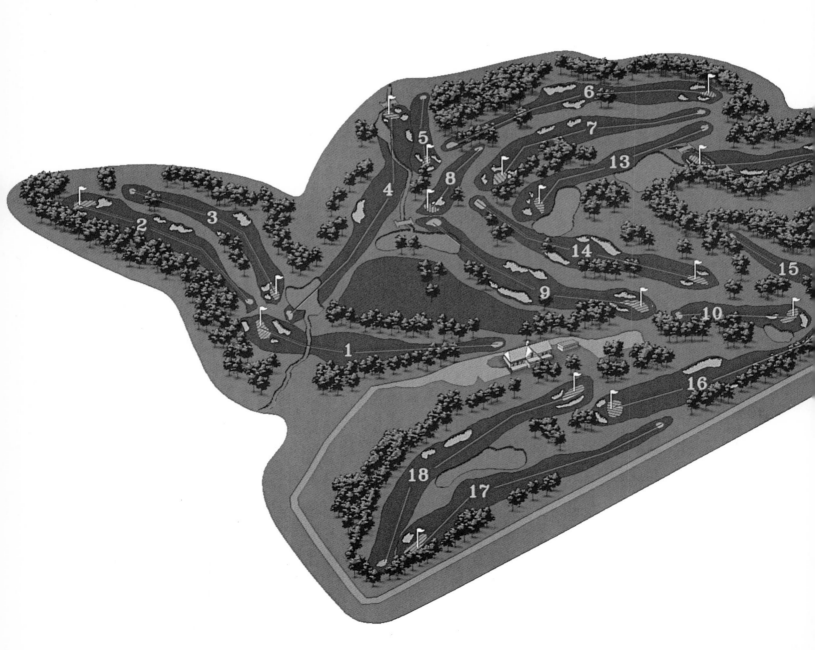

The par-three 10th marks the beginning of some of Canada's most challenging golf holes.

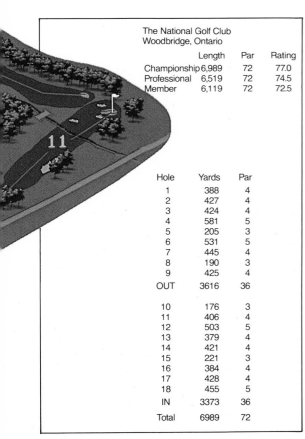

The National Golf Club
Woodbridge, Ontario

	Length	Par	Rating
Championship	6,989	72	77.0
Professional	6,519	72	74.5
Member	6,119	72	72.5

Hole	Yards	Par
1	388	4
2	427	4
3	424	4
4	581	5
5	205	3
6	531	5
7	445	4
8	190	3
9	425	4
OUT	3616	36
10	176	3
11	406	4
12	503	5
13	379	4
14	421	4
15	221	3
16	384	4
17	428	4
18	455	5
IN	3373	36
Total	6989	72

overhanging willow left.

The 11th hole provides no time to gather your wits, representing what must be one of the best par-fours in Canada. Hitting a long straight drive between bunkers right, and a hillside of tangled rough on the left, leaves a short- to mid-iron over a narrow creek into a large, undulating green. Keep in mind that the greenside rough at the National is akin to that at the U.S. Open, just the way Blechman wanted it.

Don't even consider cutting the corner on the next hole, a 500-yard, double-dogleg par-five, since accomplishing that near-impossible feat would involve carrying a stand of towering pine trees. Respect this as a true three-shot hole, laying up on your second effort. The river describes the left boundary of this beauty until it slashes across the fairway just in front of the sinister, multi-leveled green. A par on this hole is a badge of honor to be displayed with pride once back in the safe confines of the clubhouse.

Number 13 provides no respite: a 360-yard par-four that requires a drive to avoid a lake and creek on the left and ruggedly inclined rough on the right. The second shot on the dogleg-left requires a short iron to a small, well-bunkered green perched beside another pond.

No mention of The National would be complete without description of the greens. Slick, treacherous, subtle, undulating: words can scarcely hint at the work that is left once the ball reaches the putting surface. The 16th hole, perhaps one of the least remarkable in terms of design, attains mythical stature within the golfing brotherhood on the merits of its green alone. Being above the hole could mean chipping back onto the green with your next shot.

The view from the highly elevated 18th tee at The National provides seldom-equalled scenic serenity. Standing in a chute formed by tall, straight pines, you survey a good portion of the course. A clear lake on the right provides a sense of tranquil beauty but, as is The National's mischievous wont, also taunts the player to cut off as much water as he dares on his tee shot on the 445-yard uphill par-five. Overly cautious hitters will find themselves in bunkers left, blocked from the green by weeping willows. The approach shot must be high and soft to ensure the ball doesn't skid over the green into what can only be characterized as wildlife habitat.

And so it goes. The unforgiving, unforgettable National demands respect. Intelligent shot selection and a smooth swing will permit not only survival, but enjoyment.

Playing The National may not be the only way to see the course. Director of Golf Ben Kern says there are viewing areas on the course for up to 50,000 spectators and the membership is receptive to hosting the right event. "The Canadian Open, of course, the World Cup or some other significant international event would be appropriate," says the former PGA Tour player. "We have a great course and a great event would certainly showcase what we have hidden here."

Thought by many to be the toughest hole on the course, the par-four 11th rewards only two perfect shots.

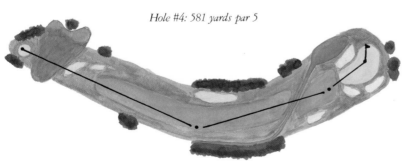

Hole #4: 581 yards par 5

Small, fast and well-protected greens are par for the National.

Most Difficult Hole

Number 4 (581 yards, par-five) A tight, twisting double dogleg that severely punishes an errant tee shot. A meandering creek bordering dense rough lurks on the right while enormous bunkers and overhanging willow trees defend the left. The creek winds across the fairway at the 150-yard mark and continues down the left side, threatening a wayward second shot. A long but narrow green is encircled by expansive bunkers, enticing the player to lay up short of the green and offer a birdie opportunity as a reward to a precise wedge.

North Halton is noted for its significant elevation changes.

NORTH HALTON

Golf and Country Club

Architect: Robert Moote
Head Professional: John Henderson
General Manager: Marion Faulkner
Superintendent: Alan Beeney

North Halton has been a golfing facility since 1914 when local realtor and businessman J.A. Willoughby hired George Cumming of the Toronto Golf Club to lay out nine holes in the Caledon Hills. Willoughby, who lived in a large house located where the present 11th tee now stands, farmed the property prior to building his course and also operated a fish hatchery in the plentiful spring-fed ponds.

A November 1919 article in Canadian Golfer magazine called this "one of the most delightful country properties to be found anywhere in the Dominion ... 128 acres of wooded uplands and stream-seamed valleys." Editor Ralph Reville went on to rhapsodize: "With a lavish hand, (Willoughby) proceeded to round it out into an ideal resort for the admirer of the artistic, the disciple of Isaac Walton and the devotee of the Royal and Ancient game."

The spectacular property was purchased by a group of businessmen in 1954 who changed the name of the course to North Halton Golf and Country Club and offered 225 shares. All were sold over a number of years and they still form the nucleus of the present shareholders.

Additional property was acquired and R.F. Moote and Associates were hired to undertake a total redesign of the course. "Bob

Moote was a part of Stanley Thompson's group of architects and you can see several Thompson characteristics in the old Moote design," says Alan Beeney, course superintendent since 1966. The 18-hole course was completed in 1969 and the club went totally private in 1974.

In 1993, the course was embarking on an extensive redesign by local architect Rene Muylaert. The seven- to eight-year project will call for the rebuilding of up to 11 greens, reconfiguring of every bunker on the course and adding others. "It's going to be quite a change from the Moote design," says Beeney. "Golfers and equipment have improved greatly in the past 25 years. Many members were hitting past the fairway traps. We never had many traps, so we wanted to add some more. Also, some of the greens may be a bit unfair and some have settled over the years."

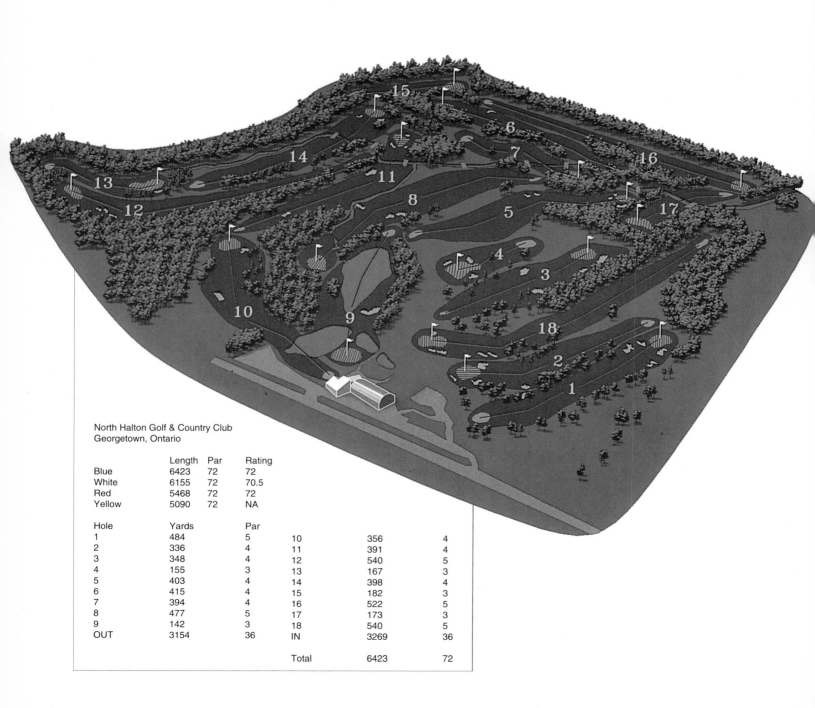

North Halton Golf & Country Club
Georgetown, Ontario

	Length	Par	Rating
Blue	6423	72	72
White	6155	72	70.5
Red	5468	72	72
Yellow	5090	72	NA

Hole	Yards	Par			
1	484	5	10	356	4
2	336	4	11	391	4
3	348	4	12	540	5
4	155	3	13	167	3
5	403	4	14	398	4
6	415	4	15	182	3
7	394	4	16	522	5
8	477	5	17	173	3
9	142	3	18	540	5
OUT	3154	36	IN	3269	36
			Total	6423	72

The 7th hole has a variety of hazards, including a creek running across the fairway.

A curling facility was built in 1960 and tennis courts and a large addition to the clubhouse were added in 1976.

Among golf cognoscenti, North Halton is known as a "sleeper." Head pro John Henderson explains: "The first four holes are open and are probably the easiest holes on the course. If you score well on these, it usually sets up your round."

From the fifth tee, the golfer is struck by the best view on the course. Almost all the valley holes can be seen from the tee. Your reverie is shortlived, however. Descending from the tee, you are challenged by the toughest holes at North Halton. "After Number 4,

you really begin to play the golf course," says Henderson. "It gets really narrow and tough." The fifth is a slight dogleg right. You tee off onto a plateau fairway which drops off about 40 feet to the left.

The sixth, a par 4 of 415 yards, is considered the most difficult hole on the course. If you want to reach the green in two shots, you have to position your drive in the narrow landing area which is guarded by evergreens on the left and evergreens and mounds on the right. The green is very elevated and slopes from right to left. "Every time I play the hole, I seem to have a different shot (because of the winds in the valley," says the pro. "I've hit a wedge in and I've hit a three-wood in."

On the seventh, big hitters need to avoid the fairway bunkers. The second shot must fly water and bunkers at front left of the green which is so deep that there is a four-club difference from front to back.

North Halton members call the second shot on Number 8 the "four or seven shot." Henderson explains: "If you don't hit the elevated green, you may find a marsh on the right or the practice range (out of bounds) on the left. If you hit the green you make four, but if you miss, you make seven."

Number 9 is a short par 3 over water but since the tee shot is made from a chute of trees, you can't really determine what effect the wind will have on your shot. The 10th yields an easy par if the drive is placed properly in the narrow landing area. Your tee shot on 11 starts you down into the valley again where, after surviving the long,

double-dogleg, par-5 12th, you can relax on 13, the easiest hole on the course.

The 14th hole may approach the difficulty of Number 6, says Henderson. "You tee off out of a chute of trees to a fairway which doglegs to the left. You then cross over the creek and hit to an elevated, narrow, well-trapped and sloping green." And on 15, the pro says, you may get to play what the members call "the pinball game." If you miss to the right of this long par 3, your ball will take more than a few bounces between the cedar trees.

Sixteen offers a straight par 5 from an elevated tee with out of bounds all the way down the left side. On the par-3 17th, you hit over a creek to an elevated kidney-shaped green, the narrowest on the course. It can play from 160 to 190 yards depending on pin placement. Number 18 is a fine finishing hole which calls for a straight drive before the hole doglegs right for the approach shot.

The wind can play havoc with a tee shot on Number 9.

Elevated tees, like this one on Number 11, are the rule at North Halton

Historic North Halton

Alas, the golden days of golf writing are mere memories, as this excerpt concerning what now is known as North Halton Golf and Country Club exemplifies. It is taken from the November 1919 issue of Canadian Golfer. "It was a glorious autumnal day, such a day as can only be found in this favored country in russet October, when Canadian Golfer motored from Hamilton over capital stone roads and through delightful scenery, some 30 miles to visit this outdoor place chosen of the gods. Color ran riot on shrub and tree and a golden haze was over the well-tilled farms and hung low on the Caledon Hills which blocked the horizon with a purple bar. ...This all too brief article is not going to tell about the wonderful trout streams and ponds; the waterscapesand landscapes, and the charm generally of this, one of the most favored spots in all Ontario, but it is going to chronicle something about the golf links, because the writer, who has played the principal courses from coast to coast, is quite convinced that from a scenic and playing standpoint they are not surpassed today on the continent."

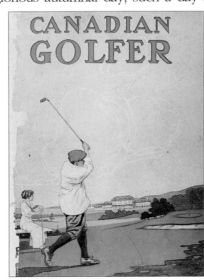

*Number 11 plays down into a valley and
then back up to a two-level green.*

ST. ANDREWS EAST

Golf and Country Club

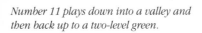

*Architect: Rene Muylaert
Founder/Director of Golf: Bill MacWilliam
Head Professional: Craig Sydorenko
Superintendent: Richard Butler*

When considering the true golf experience, the quality of the club
is as important as that of the course itself. At St. Andrew's, the
founders' intent was to create the best experience possible. They
have remained true to that credo since the successful member-
owned facility opened in 1988.

"We wanted to create a situation that we would like for our-
selves as golfers," recalls co-founder Bill MacWilliam. MacWilliam
comes by his innate understanding of golf honestly, indeed, almost
genetically: he is a third-generation golf professional. His partner
is Dave Paterson, son of prominent Canadian golf businessman
Herb Paterson, and a principal in Jim Morrison Ltd., Canada's
leading golf equipment distributors.

In their pursuit of quality over quantity, MacWilliam and Paterson
built a modest, well-appointed and efficient clubhouse designed to
serve the needs of the 350 members, and not those of tournament
participants. Outside tournaments have no place because they
interfere with the members' enjoyment of their course and St.
Andrew's doesn't need the inconvenience. The club is a model of
financial solidity and reserved tee times are unheard of.

St. Andrew's sits atop the highest point of land between Lake

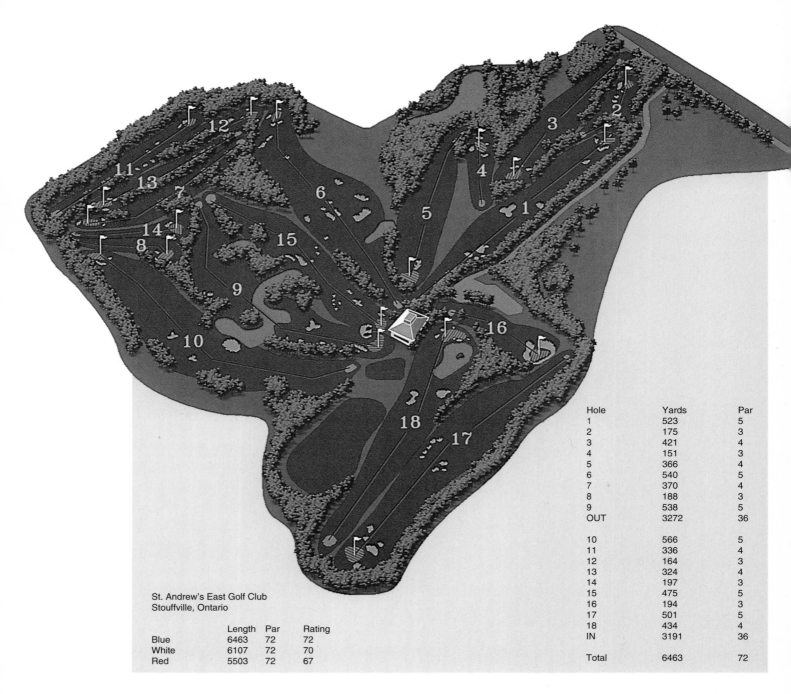

St. Andrew's East Golf Club
Stouffville, Ontario

	Length	Par	Rating
Blue	6463	72	72
White	6107	72	70
Red	5503	72	67

Hole	Yards	Par
1	523	5
2	175	3
3	421	4
4	151	3
5	366	4
6	540	5
7	370	4
8	188	3
9	538	5
OUT	3272	36
10	566	5
11	336	4
12	164	3
13	324	4
14	197	3
15	475	5
16	194	3
17	501	5
18	434	4
IN	3191	36
Total	6463	72

Ontario and Lake Simcoe northeast of Toronto. The layout, designed by Canadian Rene Muylaert with copious input from MacWilliam, is unconventional in that it features six par 3s, six par 4s and six par 5s. MacWilliam explains: "This concept avoids having long par 4s, yet still provides a course of sufficient length. The majority of players have trouble with long par 4s and we came up with a solution that makes St. Andrew's enjoyable for all the members."

Myriad bunkers, acres of fescue grass and natural flowering plants, elevation changes and precise landing areas make St. Andrew's a "target golf" situation. Since 1990, more than 3,600 trees have been added to enhance the chal-

lenge. The extensive practice facility was one of the first areas of the course to be designed and is carefully thought out, even to the northwest orientation which avoids the sun glaring into the player's eyes.

The rolling fairway of the first hole offers the first temptation of the round. On this relatively short par 5, a long drive down the middle presents the option of going for the green in two. This green is extremely well guarded by bunkers, including one with a fescue-covered island in it. Most players would be well advised to lay up on the second shot.

Number 2 is extremely deceptive, "the toughest par 3 on the course," MacWilliam says. A deep bunker on the front left and a small pot bunker on the right gobble errant shots. Most members call the par-4 third hole the toughest on the course. (See sidebar)

The par-3 fourth hole plays shorter than the card indicates since the green is some 50 feet below the tee. Savour the panoramic view of miles of surrounding forest and farmland before hitting into the three-level green sandwiched between water and forest. After surviving the first four holes, you will understand why the fifth is called "Breather." Although this mid-length par 4 is uphill, the landing area is generous and the green receptive: a birdie opportunity.

The sixth hole is a classic: the split fairway and 21 separate bunkers punish the indecisive or inaccurate player. Hitting the right-hand landing area off the tee provides a preferable angle into the green. The second shot from here must carry a vast expanse of knee-deep wildflowers. A long, accurate drive is rewarded on Number 7, a tricky par 4, since the hole gradually opens up the farther it gets from the tee. The par-3 eighth features an elevated green which is flanked by a vast, deep bunker on the right.

The ninth hole is a strong par 5 with everything: water, bunkers, trees, fescue and input from the original St. Andrews — a double green which is shared with the 15th hole. "I'm a traditionalist in many ways," says MacWilliam. "I guess this was my way of complementing the name St. Andrews. As in everything here, we've tried to remain true to the original motives of golf."

The back nine starts with a severe dog-leg left par 5 that puts the emphasis on the

Hit it as far as you can on 18 and you may have a chance of carrying the pond on your second shot.

Like many holes at St. Andrew's, the par-4 13th rewards an accurate tee shot.

tee shot. On the right, water and a multitude of bunkers, including a monster with fescue-dotted islands, forces the play left. The second shot is to a deep valley just short of the green, setting up a high pitch into a long narrow green.

Number 11 is memorable for its view from the tee and for the shallow pot bunkers lining the fairway. A long iron is recommended for position from the elevated tee. The approach to the two-tiered green must be accurate to avoid trees, out of bounds on the left and a wooded hillside on the right. The 12th is a pretty, well-treed par 3 with a tee shot likened to "shooting through goalposts."

White birches line both sides of the 13th hole and extend behind the green. A long iron into the valley sets up a high approach shot into a receptive green. Recent renovations on 14 have created a tee all but hidden by trees. This is largest green on the course; miss it right and you will face a recovery shot from a bunker 21 feet below the putting surface.

MacWilliam calls Number 15 the prettiest hole on the course. This double-dogleg into the double green is dominated by bunkers

and water threatens the tee shot. The shortest par 5 here, it represents a birdie opportunity for the player who avoids the plentiful trouble. A large green encircled by sand suggests the name "Oasis" for the 16th hole. "Depending on the wind, this hole calls for anything from a 7 iron to a driver," MacWilliam advises.

The penultimate hole at St. Andrew's is called "Funnel," appropriate since the fairway narrows almost to nothing in front of the very shallow green. Although it is a short par 5, going for the green in two calls for threading the needle. The 18th is the longest par 4 here and the key is to drive the ball as far as possible, providing you with the best chance of carrying the water in front of the green. Don't despair if your ball lands on the island in the pond: a small boat is provided for you to row out and play from there!

In 1991, MacWilliam and Paterson opened St. Andrew's Valley, a 7,300-yard beauty west of the first course. Marked by its massive mounding and expansive practice facility, the Valley course is open to the public.

The Toughest Hole at St. Andrew's

Bill MacWilliam, director of golf, says most members identify the third hole as the toughest. "This hole punishes a short fade, which is what most golfers hit. In order to do well on this hole, you must hit a draw, since the ball will bounce and roll right. Hit a fairway wood off the tee to avoid the lateral water hazard on the right and the steep hillside on the left. You will be hitting a long iron into the large, elevated, two-tiered green surrounded by fescue. Don't stray right of the green or the ball will be gone down a steep bank."

A three-tiered green on Number 4 compensates for its length.

— Toronto, Ontario —

ST. GEORGE'S

Golf and Country Club

Architect: Stanley Thompson
Head Professional: Neil Verwey
Manager: Patricia Mann
Superintendent: John Gall

The seclusion of St. George's Golf and Country Club, an oasis of calm tucked out of sight near one of Toronto busiest thoroughfares, represents in many ways the sum of all that is wonderful about golf. Ironically, St. George's owes its beginnings to Toronto's bustling atmosphere: it was originally opened to provide recreation for guests at the city's then-remarkable Royal York Hotel. The course was called the Royal York Golf Club from its inception in 1928 until 1946, when its financial arrangement ended with the Canadian Pacific Railway, owners of the hotel.

Astutely, the founders invited Stanley Thompson of Toronto, recognized as one of the premier course architects in the world at the time, to design 18 holes on the convoluted, heavily treed acreage. Thompson fulfilled his mandate admirably, producing a layout that has stood the test of time as very few other courses have. Head Professional Neil Verwey cites one of Thompson's commandments when he says, "The golf course fits the terrain. It doesn't have that 'manufactured' feel to it that a lot of new ones do.

"Each hole is unique unto itself," says Verwey. "There is no sameness to any of the holes at St. George's. The course is very

Stanley Thompson's classic layout has stood the test of time.

playable. The landing areas aren't tight, but you have to be very careful with your second shots and by no means are you finished once you get to the green. The par-threes here are fantastic and, of course, it has Thompson's thumbprint, which is his great fairway bunkers."

Four Canadian Opens were played on Thompson's classic layout: 1933 (won by Joe Kirkwood), 1949 (E.J. Harrison), 1960 (Art Wall) and 1968 (Bob Charles). In addition, St. George's has been a favored site for the du Maurier Ltd. Classic, designated as one of the four "major" events on the Ladies' Professional Golf Association Tour. Two-time winner JoAnne Carner (1975, 1978) says it is "the best club I have ever played; no four finer finishing holes in the world." After her second win, she commented that the final round was "the

St. George's Golf and Country Club
Toronto, Ontario

	Length	Par	Rating
Blue	6797	71	73
White	6477	71	71
Red	6205	71	69.5

Hole	Yards	Par			
1	378	4	10	377	4
2	420	4	11	517	5
3	201	3	12	383	4
4	480	5	13	214	3
5	403	4	14	446	4
6	146	3	15	580	5
7	442	4	16	203	3
8	217	3	17	447	4
9	543	5	18	400	4
OUT	3230	35	IN	3567	36
			Total	6797	71

greatest round I ever played on the toughest course I ever played." In total, St. George's played host to five du Maurier Ltd. Classics between 1975 and 1984.

Playing the course like the LPGA stars would be too much to ask, but here are a few notes from the hole-by-hole commentary prepared for the event: "The first hole is one of the finer opening holes in golf. From an elevated tee, the golfer plays to a roomy but sloping fairway. The second shot will be about 130 yards to a slightly elevated green. The prevailing wind quarters left to right. The second hole is one of the tougher holes because of the undulating terrain. The tee shot is from one elevation to another and the fairway slopes to the right. The approach will be about 180 yards to a green protected by a boundary on the left and bunkers right. The green is long and narrow, demanding precision and control from the two-iron to five-wood second shot. The third is another elevated tee shot, but the big problem here is the narrow and severely sloping green. Though the shot will be something like a three-iron, the green won't be too difficult to hit, sitting as it does so receptively below the player. But once on the green, the player will have to take care."

The finishing holes have claimed their share of competitors, the hole-by-hole commentary notes in its description of the 14th. "By now, the hills may be taking their toll on players, but anyone who can hang in there will be in good shape. Pars are the thing on these holes in the middle of the back side. Golfers will likely flirt with the left side of the fairway,

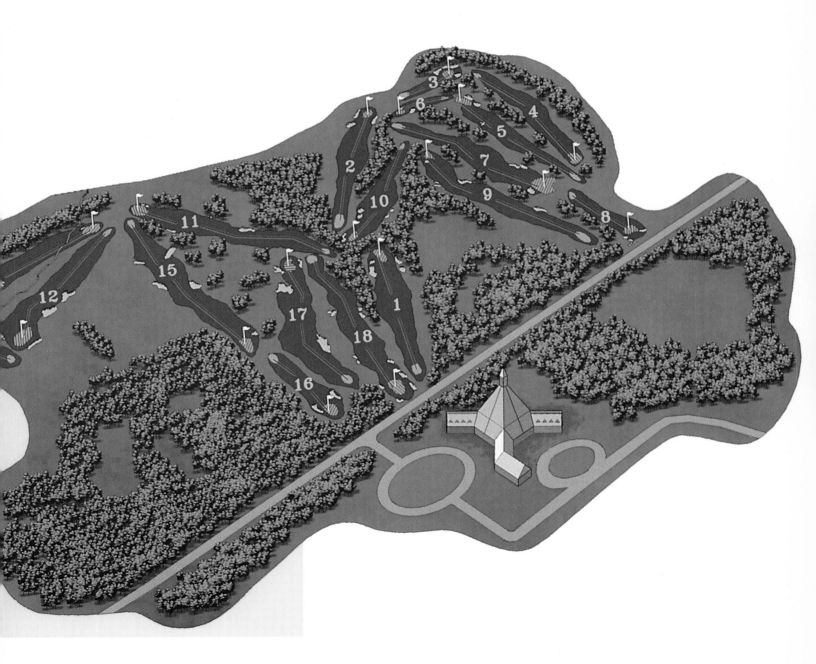

St. George's features excellent par-fours. On the 446-yard 14th, the second shot must clear the creek.

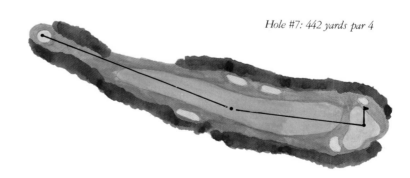

Hole #7: 442 yards par 4

The Toughest Hole at St. George's

The Number 1-rated stroke hole at St. George's Golf and Country Club is the par-four seventh hole which plays 442 yards from the blue tees and 20 yards less from the whites. Head Pro Neil Verwey respectfully suggests that you "grunt" on your tee shot. "You've got to hit the ball as far and straight as you can. Even then, you'll still be facing a long-iron or fairway wood into a very severe green. There are fairway traps and mounds all the way up the left side, and trees on both sides — and it's all uphill. Your second shot has to carry bunkers in front of the green. A super hole."

but this is the blind side from the tee. Still, those who succeed in placing their ball will have a shorter club for the second shot. It is a give-and-take hole, for the second shot from the left side will contend with a green banked on the right by a hill, and directly in line with the player's approach. The 15th is some kind of hole! After two shots down a fairway reminiscent of the first, the golfer is left with a shot up to the clouds. The green is so raised that it seems the shot is a pop fly, but it is a very difficult green to work with, angling on the front and back right.

"What a challenge these final holes are," the commentary continues. "The 16th hole takes the golfer to the perimeter of the course, not far from where she began, and offers the first of a variety of testing shots down the last stretch. Here is a green with a narrow entrance, a deep bunker right and trees left. A high fade is the shot, but that's a bit of a challenge with a long-iron. Number 17 is a slight dogleg-right where the long hitter does

have an advantage: she can try to shave yards by cutting the corner. That will leave a four- or five-iron to a well-trapped green cut on an angle. To the right is a gully and a bunker demanding a shot from eight feet down.

"Nothing like a finishing hole that leads toward a rambling old clubhouse in the distance," the summary concludes. "Victory may seem within grasp, but the approach is fraught with problems. A bunker at the left front and another at the right corner make the second shot hard on the nerves. Even if the bunkers are avoided, there is always the chance of the next being played from the sidehill lie in rough that fringes the green and bunkers. As usual, the green will be quick, and so this final hole will epitomize all that is best about St. George's as a site for a major championship: it demands the full shot mixed with the delicate touch, the knowledge to hit a variety of shots, and the good sense to know when to apply that knowledge. It demands restraint, finesse and strength."

Many championships have been decided on the 18th green: four Canadian Opens and five du Maurier Ltd. Classics among them.

Weston is famous for its treacherous greens, such as this one on the par-four fifth hole.

WESTON

Golf and Country Club

Architect: Willie Park Jr.
Head Professional: Herb Holzscheiter
Manager: Michael Jory
Superintendent: Thom Charters

The Weston Golf and Country Club is best known as the site of Arnold Palmer's first professional victory. While Palmer's win at the 1955 Canadian Open at Weston was a memorable occasion, it is not the sole reason the course is recognized as one of Canada's best.

Weston was founded in 1914 following a town-hall meeting at which local businessmen decided to rent land in the nearby Humber Valley to construct a course. Initially, they built a crude four-hole course which served as an adventurous but adequate start. The area also served as a pasture and one of the first problems was keeping grazing cattle off the greens.

With a growing membership, the course soon expanded to nine holes and Percy Barrett, who had been an assistant to the famous Harry Vardon in Britain and runner-up in the first Canadian Open in 1904, was hired as the first professional.

Barrett was a strict disciplinarian. One day, when he was about to hit his drive off the first tee, he wheeled around and pointed his finger at a caddie. "You were talking," accused Barrett. "No sir, I was not talking," the caddie boldly replied. "Well," said the gruff Barrett, "you were going to."

In 1921, the club purchased the land it had been renting, as well as some surrounding acreage, and hired Willie Park Jr., a noted Scottish architect who twice had won the British Open, to design an 18-hole layout. The design was well-received and, with the war over, applications for membership came in droves. The fees for 1921 were set at $60 for gentlemen and $30 for ladies. In 1922, the course was opened officially with much pomp that included an exhibition match with English professionals Sandy Taylor and Alex Herd taking on Barrett and 1905 Canadian Open champion George Cumming of the Toronto Golf Club.

While the course has remained virtually unchanged from Park's admirable original design, nature has forced a few alterations. Most of those have come at the spectacular second hole, now a 314-yard par-four that has become the course's signature. Players tee off from a precipice 120 feet above a fairway bounded on the right by a pond and on the left by rough and trees. The green sits at the foot of a towering railway trestle which dominates the landscape.

In the past, however, this hole was a par-three, only to be destroyed by the flooding of the Humber River during Hurricane Hazel four decades ago. For a time, it became a lengthy par-four with a green on the far side of the trestle. The players' challenge was to decide whether to go under or over the ominous structure.

Anyone who plays Weston for the first time is struck by the immaculate conditioning, another trademark of the course. The 6,698-yard layout is kept in impeccable shape and possesses lightning-fast greens. In fact, veteran PGA Tour star Raymond Floyd has compared their speed with that at major championships such as The Masters. The greens are, for the most part, small and very deceiving. Scoring well at Weston requires patience and a smooth stroke on the greens.

Weston is a traditional course in every sense

Weston Golf and Country Club Weston, Ontario			
	Length	Par	Rating
Blue	6698	72	72
White	6465	72	71
Yellow	5889	74	73

Hole	Yards	Par
1	413	4
2	314	4
3	472	5
4	156	3
5	424	4
6	385	4
7	571	5
8	131	3
9	448	4
OUT	3314	36
10	337	4
11	235	3
12	471	5
13	376	4
14	438	4
15	192	3
16	541	5
17	350	4
18	444	4
IN	3384	36
Total	6698	72

of the word. The majority of holes are lined with maple, oak and spruce trees from tee to green, and a level stance on the fairways is a rare treat. The course ebbs and flows with many natural changes in elevation and scenery. There are no gimmicks at Weston; what you see is what you get.

A linkage of three holes — the fifth, sixth and seventh — provide one of the best tests of golf in Canada, and many a match has been won or lost here despite their early appearance in the round. The first two are long par-fours with danger lurking on both sides of their fairways. Both are remarkable for their extremely difficult greens that require precision placement of approach shots and careful study of the resulting putts. Ending up on the wrong side of the pin almost certainly assures a disastrous three-putt. The last in this tough trio is a tremendous 571-yard par-five with the tee set back in a tree-lined chute. To have any chance of reaching the green in two shots,

The eighth hole, although only 131 yards long, yields more bogies than birdies.

players must power a drive to the top of a knoll which cuts across the fairway. Being short of the crest can result in a blind second shot, the outcome being a bogey, or worse.

Weston's 18th hole presents a challenging completion to a round. A 444-yard par-four, the downhill dogleg-left plays shorter than its yardage indicates, but requires a brilliant tee shot. The green rarely holds anything but a superb approach and a bump-and-run strategy is often best. Once there, heed the members' credo that all putts break to the clubhouse, although you'll be hard pressed to do so since your eyes tend to deceive you on this subtle putting surface.

Weston has an impressive tournament history. In addition to the 1955 Canadian Open, it has played host to the 1971 Ontario Open, won by the late George Knudson, and Ontario Amateurs in 1964 and 1978, both won by Gary Cowan. In 1990, to honor its 75th anniversary, the club opened its doors to the Cadillac Classic skins game, featuring Palmer, Floyd, Mark Calcavecchia and eventual winner Dave Barr of Richmond, B.C. The year was capped by the hosting of the Canadian Amateur championship, won, fittingly, by Weston member Warren Sye.

Weston is perennially rated one of the best conditioned courses in Canada.

The 16th hole with its elevated green plays even longer than the 541 yards on the card.

Birth of a Legend

In 1955, a 25-year-old rookie professional named Arnold Palmer had his back to the wall. He had been shut out on the PGA Tour despite winning the U.S. Amateur the previous year and had enough money to last just six more weeks on tour. Coming to Weston Golf and Country Club to face a stellar field for the Canadian Open, he couldn't be blamed for feeling despondent. "I was frustrated with my play," Palmer recalls. "I felt I had been playing well, but I wasn't getting any results." But playing on a rain-soaked course that yielded low scores, Palmer sat in second place after the first round, firing a 64 to trail Charley Sifford by a shot. He improved on that standing the following day, shooting 67 to take the lead. The third round, he achieved another 64 in a curious manner: three shots that appeared headed for the woods caromed back into play after hitting spectators. At 21 under par after three rounds, Palmer coasted through the final day with a 70. The winner's cheque for $2,400 staked him on his way to becoming one of the best golfers of all time.

Water in front of the 12th green has swallowed many an approach shot.

MILL RIVER

Provincial Golf Course

Architect: C.E. (Robbie) Robinson
Head Professional: Steve Dowling
General Manager: Greg McKee
Superintendent: Blair Duggan

Mill River Golf Course has been called "one of the sternest tests of golf in Eastern Canada," and has proven it time and again, in Canadian Tour events, the Canadian Junior Championship and provincial tournaments. Opened in 1971, this course was picked by SCORE Magazine in 1989 as one of the top public courses in the country and stretches to more than 6,800 yards from the back tees.

Like its notable Island neighbors, Brudenell and Green Gables, Mill River is owned and operated by the provincial government and is open to the public. Tee times can be reserved up to nine days in advance. Not only is the golf course first-rate, but it is adjacent to the Rodd Mill River Resort, complete with dining and convention facilities, indoor aquaplex with a 20-metre pool, two squash courts, a 95-foot water slide and Nautilus room. Camping is also available in the park which features a marina and children's fun park.

Listen while head pro Steve Dowling, who has been at Mill River for 12 years, plays each hole. "Number 1 is a short, 90-degree dogleg left. It's best to hit a four- or five-iron off the tee to the rise of the hill. A long drive could find two traps or go into the woods.

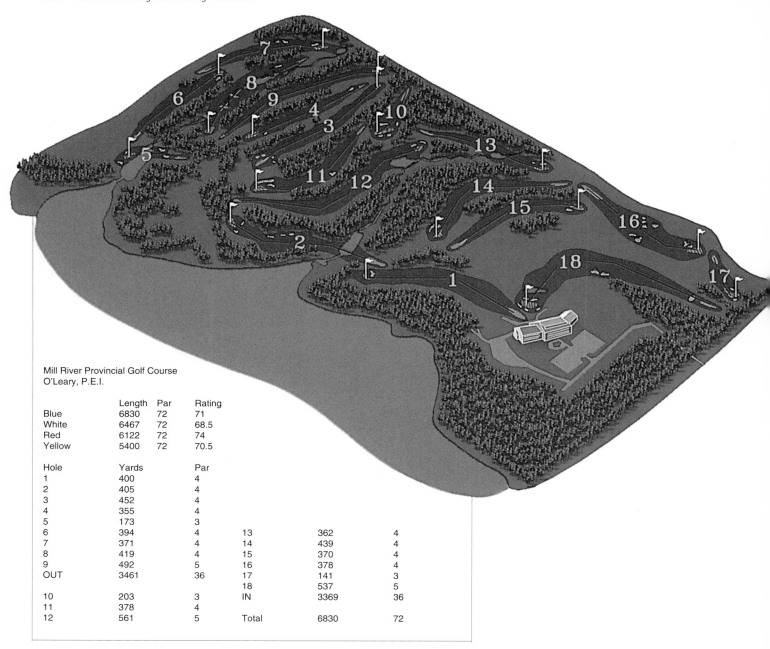

Mill River Provincial Golf Course
O'Leary, P.E.I.

	Length	Par	Rating
Blue	6830	72	71
White	6467	72	68.5
Red	6122	72	74
Yellow	5400	72	70.5

Hole	Yards	Par			
1	400	4			
2	405	4			
3	452	4			
4	355	4			
5	173	3			
6	394	4	13	362	4
7	371	4	14	439	4
8	419	4	15	370	4
9	492	5	16	378	4
OUT	3461	36	17	141	3
			18	537	5
10	203	3	IN	3369	36
11	378	4			
12	561	5	Total	6830	72

You will be left with an eight- or nine-iron into a two-tiered green. There are sand traps to the right of the green and the pin is often set behind them.

"The second hole is a very tough par 4 with an elevated tee. Your drive must carry water for the first 120 yards. Mill River bounds part of the left side of the fairway and there are trees on the right. Usually a three- or five-wood off the tee with an eight- or nine-iron approach.

"Number 3 is a long, tough par 4 with a tree in the middle of the fairway. The fairway is lined by trees on both sides and behind the green. The green is flat with no elevation, so it's very difficult to judge the distance on your second shot. An accurate tee shot with a driver will still leave most golfers with a fairway wood to get home. Even if you do get on in three, you're still not finished because of the very large two-tiered green.

"The fourth is a very tight par 4, but it's short. Hit anything from a five-iron to a three-wood off the tee. A well-placed drive will leave you with a short iron into a green guarded by mounds that will kick balls into the woods.

"Number 5 is a very pretty par 3. The tee is elevated above the water and you're hitting a seven- or eight-iron to a very large two-tiered green, with mounds and bunkers at the back. Take enough club because the water reaches around to the front of the green.

"The sixth is a par 4 with an island of trees in the middle of the fairway. There is out of bounds on the left and trees on the right. If you hit driver off the tee, your second shot is a blind six- or seven-iron over the island of trees. You want to be on the same level as the pin on the three-tiered green or you may three-putt.

"Number 7 is a dogleg right with many contours and dips in the fairway. There is a gully about 150 yards out, so your goal with the driver is to get over the gully and up onto the rise. You will be left with a mid-iron to the green which is guarded by two bunkers." Dowling picks the eighth hole as the toughest on the course (see sidebar).

He says the par-5 ninth "is an easy hole in length but a very hard hole with lots of woods and lots of rough." Once again, there is a three-tiered green. The par-3 10th requires a four- or five-iron into a green that slopes significantly from right to left. And the par-4 11th is a short dogleg right, once again cut out of the dense bush. Dowling describes the 11th as looking like it was "cut out of the forest with a cookie cutter." Hit a fairway wood or long iron off the tee and you will be left with a short iron into another three-tiered green.

The 12th is a very pretty hole with its left side lined by trees and with water in front of the green to challenge players who try to

Leave the driver in the bag on Number 4.

*The course's namesake — Mill River
— comes into play on the par-4
second hole.*

hit the green in two. The teeing ground on the par-4 13th is set back in a chute of trees and, if the tees are up, the gambler will attempt to carry the pond in the fairway. Most, however, will tee off with an eight-iron and then hit a four-iron to an elevated green. "Never be above the hole here or it's an automatic three-putt," says Dowling.

Both 14 and 15 are par-4 doglegs to the left. Number 14 is the tougher of the two because the hole turns 90 degrees. Hit three-wood off the tee and then a five-wood or long iron in. The 16th is the first hole on Mill River that is out in the open. "It's really the first opportunity for the golfer to pull the driver out of the bag and let loose," says the pro. The second shot will be a seven- or eight-iron. Seventeen is a short par 3 that requires anything from a nine-iron to a four-iron.

The par-5 finishing hole at Mill River rewards a long drive. Err to the right because there is out of bounds left, and you will be left with a fairway wood or long iron into a huge, well-bunkered green. "It's a great opportunity to finish with a birdie and leave Mill River with a smile on your face," Dowling concludes.

Mill River, combined with the other existing courses and the new Links at Crowbush Cove, re-emphasizes that Prince Edward Island's combination of hospitality, seafood and golf ranks it among the world's premier golf destinations.

The Toughest Hole at Mill River

Mill River's eighth hole, a 419-yard par 4 bisected by a string of 11 spring-fed ponds, is the toughest on the course, according to head professional Steve Dowling. "Visitors get there and they just don't know what to do. The way I play it depends on the risk or the reward. There's more fairway on the left side, but then it's a tougher second shot in. If you hit a three-wood to the small landing area on the right, you can flip a wedge straight across for a much easier shot. If I'm out there and I'm four over, I'll go down the right side. If I'm under par, I'll usually chicken out and go left. Even if you hit a real good tee shot, you still have to face the elevated green. It's a great golf hole."

The prudent player will lay up short of the water off the 13th tee.

ROYAL MONTREAL

Golf Club

Architect: Dick Wilson
Head Professional: Bob Hogarth
Manager: Denzil Palmer
Superintendent: Ron Leishman

The early days of the history of golf in Canada are almost synonymous with the Royal Montreal Golf Club — the oldest golf club in North America, beating Royal Quebec onto the scene by a mere six months back in 1873. Royal Montreal's ground-breaking efforts didn't cease for decades. It was the first Canadian club to receive the "Royal" prefix (in 1884), the first in Canada to import an English golf professional (William Davis in 1881), the first on the continent to allow women members (1891), and it played host to the very first Canadian Open in 1904.

Now into its second century, the history of Royal Montreal is intertwined with that of the early settlement of this country. Golf had been played in the Montreal area by early fur traders, and a notice dating back 50 years prior to the founding of Royal Montreal invites members of the city's Scots community to a golf outing west of town. That the evolutionary process would continue to its inevitable outcome might not have been obvious in those days, although it is to those looking back.

The historic event came to pass on November 4, 1873, in the office of the Sidey Brothers, prominent Montreal businessmen. One of the founding members was Alexander Dennistoun, who served

as the first president and captain of Royal Montreal until 1890. The original site, called Fletcher's Field, was on the flank of Mount Royal and boasted six holes, which were probably sufficient for the 25 members. By 1895, the growth of both the city and the membership necessitated a move to the outskirts of Montreal.

Longtime members fondly recall this so-called "Dixie" site on the bank of the St. Lawrence River in what now is the westend suburb of Dorval. By 1922, this course featured 36 holes — the famed North and South layouts — designed by Willie Park Jr., architect of other fine Canadian layouts such as Weston Golf and Country Club and Calgary Golf and Country Club. The second of two clubhouses built on this location, and completed the same year as Park's courses, was widely acknowledged as the finest in Canada.

In 1957, Royal Montreal moved for the final time to a 650-acre site on a beautiful island called Ile Bizard northwest of Montreal. The club engaged Florida architect Dick Wilson, whose work on West Palm Beach Country Club in Florida and NCR Country Club in Ohio made him one of the most sought-after course designers of that era, to build two 18-hole courses at the new site. Wilson was suitably impressed by the club's choice of property. "The great feature of this place," he said, "is the great sweep of the landscape. That vista of the Lake of Two Mountains is the perfect backdrop to these courses."

Head Professional Bruce Murray knows the courses as well as anyone and admires the Wilson design. "A general feature of the Royal Montreal courses," he has said, "a tendency of Dick Wilson, is that the bunkering of all the holes is more apparent on the front of the green and the entrances are very narrow. The key is that bunkers are positioned very close to the putting surface, which makes Royal Montreal basically a second-shot layout. You've got to hit the ball up onto the green, so the premium is on accuracy."

Royal Montreal is often thought of as possessing only 18 holes — the renowned Blue course that played host to the Canadian Open in 1975 and 1980. Many golfers do not realize there are 27 other holes at Ile Bizard. "The Red course is just as good or better than the Blue," says Murray. "It may not be as spectacular because there is no water, but it is just as tight and testing. In many ways, it's similar to Scotland. The 13th and 14th holes, for example, have high mounds and well-bunkered greens. The fifth hole on the Red is an exceptional par-four — the Number 1 stroke hole. And Number 10 is a long, strong par-three with lots of sand and a narrow entrance to the green." As well, Murray points out that the so-called "Dixie" nine, which plays to 3,100 yards, is a collection of good holes that is often overlooked.

The Blue course is generally considered the tournament course. The group of the final four holes is acknowledged as one of the toughest

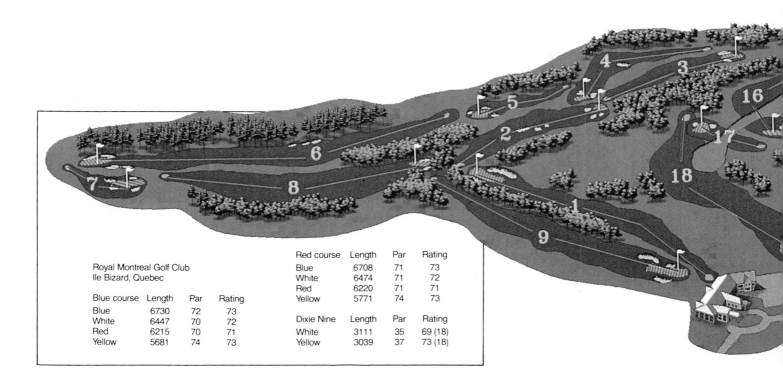

Royal Montreal Golf Club				Red course	Length	Par	Rating
Ile Bizard, Quebec				Blue	6708	71	73
				White	6474	71	72
				Red	6220	71	71
Blue course	Length	Par	Rating	Yellow	5771	74	73
Blue	6730	72	73				
White	6447	70	72	Dixie Nine	Length	Par	Rating
Red	6215	70	71	White	3111	35	69 (18)
Yellow	5681	74	73	Yellow	3039	37	73 (18)

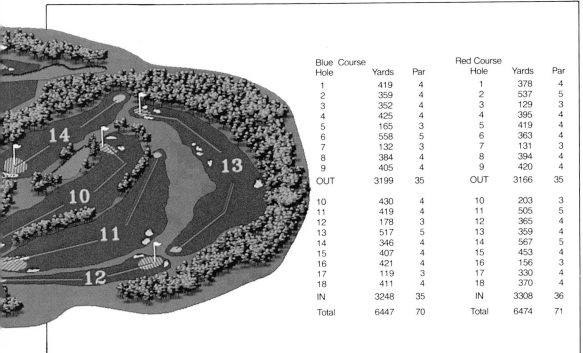

The 16th hole on Royal Montreal's Blue Course has been called one of the best par-fours in the country.

Blue Course			Red Course		
Hole	Yards	Par	Hole	Yards	Par
1	419	4	1	378	4
2	359	4	2	537	5
3	352	4	3	129	3
4	425	4	4	395	4
5	165	3	5	419	4
6	558	5	6	363	4
7	132	3	7	131	3
8	384	4	8	394	4
9	405	4	9	420	4
OUT	3199	35	OUT	3166	35
10	430	4	10	203	3
11	419	4	11	505	5
12	178	3	12	365	4
13	517	5	13	359	4
14	346	4	14	567	5
15	407	4	15	453	4
16	421	4	16	156	3
17	119	3	17	330	4
18	411	4	18	370	4
IN	3248	35	IN	3308	36
Total	6447	70	Total	6474	71

tests in Canada. Number 15, a 400-yard par-four with the wind generally following, may dictate a fairway wood off the tee, for a well-struck drive could end up in the lake. Hit a seven- or eight-iron over the water but make sure you take enough club to get to the green. The reason? Royal Montreal's greens feature narrow throats with heavy frontal bunkering. "You can hit to the middle or back of the greens here all day," says Murray, "and not get into trouble. Just don't be short, otherwise you'll have little puff shots over bunkers on every hole and those can wear you out in a hurry."

The 16th is "as good a par-four as there is in Canada," says Murray. The lake runs the length of the left side, so the better player will try to cut the ball in over the lake to the centre of the fairway. He still faces a four- or five-iron uphill and over a pond. Number 17 is a great par-three: caught between the water and a large bunker left is a small green that narrows severely at the entrance. Only a short-iron effort at 120 yards, this hole can wreak psychological and physical damage.

The finishing hole is a splendid par-four with an interesting tournament history. Jack Nicklaus, with a one-shot lead over Tom Weiskopf in the 1975 Open, splashed his one-iron effort into water at the corner of the dogleg. Although his heroic third shot (after taking a penalty) reached the green and he salvaged a bogey, Weiskopf made par to force the playoff which Nicklaus lost.

The Red Course at Royal Montreal: the par-three 10th hole requires length and accuracy.

The short 17th on the Blue Course severely punishes an errant tee shot.

Charlie Murray

History, of Course

Another Royal Montreal claim to fame is that only five head professionals, three of them with the surname Murray, have been employed here in 110 years.

Willie Davis was brought to the original site in 1881. (Recent research indicates it may have been Davis, not Willie Dunn, who designed historic Shinnecock Hills in the United States after he left Royal Montreal.) The others were Charlie Murray, a two-time Canadian Open champion, and his son Kenny.

The present head professional, Bruce Murray (no relation to Charley and Kenny), took over after Pat Fletcher, remembered as the last Canadian to win our national championship in 1954. But Jack Young holds the individual record: he served as an assistant professional here for more than 50 years!

Meticulous attention to detail makes Riverside one of the most attractive courses in the country.

——————— *Saskatoon, Saskatchewan* ———————

RIVERSIDE

Country Club

Architect: William Kinnear
Head Professional: Larry Ewanyshyn
Executive-Director: Don Campbell
Superintendent: Doug Campbell

If your image of the province of Saskatchewan is one of barren expanses of monotonous prairie trailing off endlessly to the horizon and beyond, then be prepared for a shock when you drive up to the entrance to the Riverside Country Club.

The name alone should give you a hint. Standing proudly on a plateau some 170 metres above the brawny Saskatchewan River, Riverside has the appearance of an oasis of calm — until you discover that its 400 male members and 150 ladies and their guests play more than 35,000 rounds in a six-month season. Those fortunate enough to set foot on its manicured fairways discover a world apart: Riverside's 18 well-designed holes wend their way through hilly, heavily treed terrain. So much for that stereotype of the Prairies . . .

Stephen Ross, executive-director of the Royal Canadian Golf Association, has visited dozens of courses coast to coast during his years with the RCGA. He calls Riverside "an exceptional golf course. Without a doubt, one of Western Canada's best courses and one of the country's best-kept secrets." Ross first visited Riverside in the late 1970s and has played it many times since. "It's one of my favorite courses anywhere. In addition to having a first-rate, well-conditioned course, it is fortunate to have a wonderful mem-

bership and top-notch management. It's almost impossible to find anything negative to say about Riverside."

The original course at Riverside Country Club was designed and built by a Scotsman named Bill Kinnear, who came to Saskatoon in 1909. Mickey Boyle's informative book, Ninety Years of Golf (An Illustrated History of Golf in Saskatchewan), notes that Kinnear was neither a professional nor a course architect. Apparently, his only qualifications were his Scottish burr and the fact that he had taken golf lessons at the Old Course at St. Andrews, Scotland. In any case, Kinnear laid out nine holes of the Saskatoon Golf Club in 1910, staying on as professional and grounds superintendent until 1946. He also designed and built the Riverside Country Club and served as the pro and superintendent there as well.

Though he didn't know it, Kinnear had started a bit of a tradition at the club. Don Campbell, the club's executive-director, has been with Riverside for an indeterminate number of years: "Let's just say I came here as a kid after the war." After dabbling at a number of jobs around the club, he wound up as its grounds superintendent. In 1969,

Abundant water and trees on the fourth hole belie many Prairie stereotypes.

when times were a little tight around the club, he agreed to add the role of general manager to his portfolio. Then he took on the food and beverage responsibilities. No wonder the RCGA's Stephen Ross refers to Campbell as "Mr. Riverside!" He has divested himself of everything but the overall management of Riverside, passing on the mantle of superintendent to his son, Doug.

With that background, Don Campbell has an encyclopedic knowledge of the club and the intricacies of the course. Kinnear's layout has stood the test of time well, although Campbell credits two outstanding Canadian architects, C.E. (Robbie) Robinson and Bill Robinson (no relation) with bringing the course to the high standard it enjoys today. "Robbie came in here in the late 1950s with a master plan that made it much better," Campbell recalls. "And then, in the early '70s, Bill's plan added the finishing touches that took us to the top. We've planted many trees, as called for by Bill's plan. We've also added flowers all over the place — we put in more than 60,000 bedding plants every year — rock gardens, retaining walls, and so on. The course is manicured to the hilt, very picturesque."

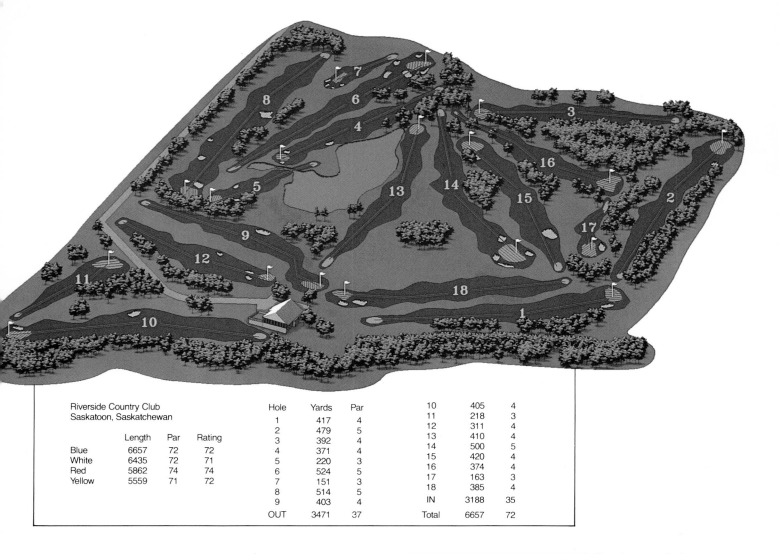

Riverside Country Club
Saskatoon, Saskatchewan

	Length	Par	Rating
Blue	6657	72	72
White	6435	72	71
Red	5862	74	74
Yellow	5559	71	72

Hole	Yards	Par
1	417	4
2	479	5
3	392	4
4	371	4
5	220	3
6	524	5
7	151	3
8	514	5
9	403	4
OUT	3471	37

Hole	Yards	Par
10	405	4
11	218	3
12	311	4
13	410	4
14	500	5
15	420	4
16	374	4
17	163	3
18	385	4
IN	3188	35
Total	6657	72

Pulling the approach shot on No. 10 means the ball will come to rest in the river valley.

Another of Bill Robinson's suggestions was a seven-acre man-made lake that comes into play on the fourth, fifth and 13th holes. The lake represents the only water on the course, with the notable exception of the Saskatchewan River which makes an appearance on the first and 10th holes, causing "a lot of trouble," says Campbell. The river forms the righthand boundary of the very difficult opening hole. "The river and the bush on its bank guard the right side," he says, "and the fairway slopes

Hole #6: 524 yards par 5

left to right. The target area is about 240 yards out on the left, leaving a five- or a six-iron in. The green is big, with a bunker on the right and out-of-bounds behind."

The river is a factor on the first hole of the back nine, as well. "The 10th is another tough hole. There's a fairway bunker out about 250 yards on the right, and the river and bush on the left. Try to aim for right-centre for the best approach. It's anything from a five- to a seven-iron in from there. The green is very tricky and has a bunker, rough and trees on the right. There's another bunker on the left, and if you're left of that, you're down the slope in the riverbottom."

The secret to getting around Riverside with a respectable score is not in hitting the ball long, but straight. The layout plays to 6,800 yards from the tips and the smart player will try to keep the ball in the fairway at all costs, even if it means gearing down from the driver off the tee. What rough there is on this neatly groomed layout is treacherous and a ball in the trees will be found, but not advanced toward the hole.

As well, the prevailing wind comes into play on the fifth hole, part of what Campbell calls the most difficult stretch on the course. It may unnerve first-time players to discover that he considers the first six holes the most challenging of Riverside's 18. After surviving the first, the par-five second hole offers a slight reprieve — maybe even a birdie. But then, in rapid succession, come the 392-yard third hole, noted as an exacting driving hole; the par-four fourth with its distracting water threatening the tee shot; the muscular 220-yard par-three fifth; and the sixth, rated the Number 1 stroke hole.

In contrast to this crucial challenge, Ross recalls several holes fondly. His favorites include the dogleg ninth hole, with its blind second shot. "It's one of the greatest short par-fours anywhere. Your drive must be left, and there's

The Toughest Hole at Riverside

The Number 1 stroke hole at Riverside Country Club in Saskatoon, Saskatchewan, is the 524-yard, par-five sixth hole. It is the longest hole on the course and, appropriately, is considered the best driving hole. To reach the green in two, you must bust your drive 270 yards and stay to the left. Your three-wood second shot must carry four traps on its way to the green. Most players will try to lay up in front of the traps, some 50 yards short of the green.

gorse left and right. Very links-style." Number 12 is another short par-four where Ross recommends a two-iron off the tee to ensure your drive avoids the punitive rough. "The 18th is a great finishing hole with a severe second shot. You've got to hit two very straight shots. You're hitting a five- or six-iron into a very elevated, narrow green. There's a slope on the right that goes down about 20 feet, and if you're down there, well, forget it."

A short par-four, the 12th will punish those who use a driver from the tee.

PHOTOGRAPHIC CREDITS

Unless otherwise noted, all photographs in this book are by Michael French. Front Cover: Doug Ball; Capilano Golf Club, 39; Cape Breton Highlands National Park, 82, 86; Greystone Golf Club, 148, 149, 151, 152, 153; Dieter Hessell, 160, 161, 162, 164, 165; Niakwa Golf Club, 69; Marc Rochelle, author photograph; Royal Canadian Golf Association Museum, 201; Royal Montreal Golf Club, 231; Score Magazine 15, 135, 207; Don Vickery, 171.

CREDITS

Computer Design and Production: Nick Pitt
Copy Editor: Leslie Gordon
Cover Design: Andrew Smith
Book Design/Art Direction: Nancy Roberts-Knox
Photography: Michael French
Golf Course Computer Art: Baynger-Northey Associate⁻
Golf Watercolours: Paul Alette
Typesetting: True to Type Inc.
Colour Separations: Colour Technologies, Toronto
Paper: Provincial Papers
Printing: D.W. Friesen, Altona, Manitoba